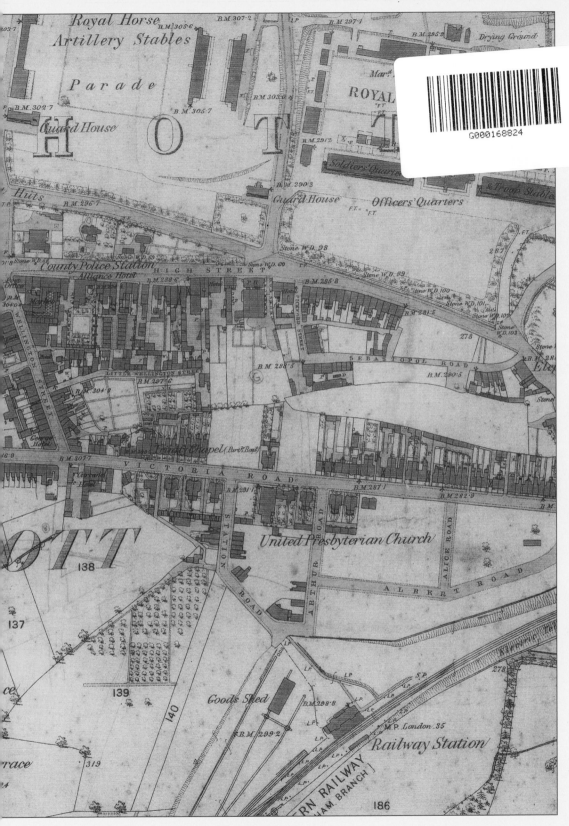

The centre of 'Aldershott' as shown on a map of 1871. It is only 17 years since the Army first arrived yet already the town has grown considerably. The railway station, bottom right, is isolated in what was open country and a lot of the area to the east of Grosvenor Road, then still known as Bank Street is still to be developed.

ALDERSHOT PAST

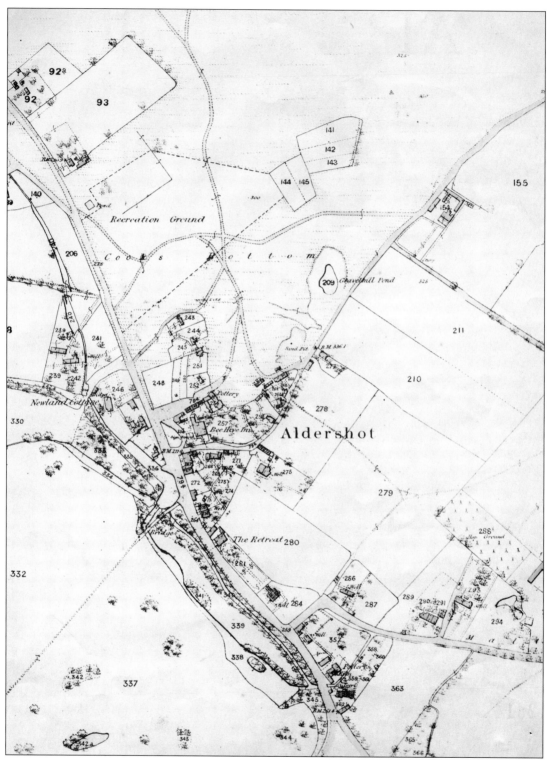

An 1855 map of Aldershot.

ALDERSHOT PAST

Stephen Phillips
&
Gillian Picken

Phillimore

2000

Published by
PHILLIMORE & CO. LTD.
Shopwyke Manor Barn, Chichester, West Sussex

ISBN 1 86077 144 0

Printed and bound in Great Britain by
BIDDLES LTD.
Guildford, Surrey

Contents

List of Illustrations

Frontispiece: Aldershot in 1855

Acknowledgements

We wish to express our sincere thanks and appreciation to all those individuals and organisations who have encouraged and helped in the production of this book. Many people have assisted in providing invaluable information without which the book would have been all the poorer; however, any errors which occur are the fault of ourselves and ourselves alone.

Members of the Aldershot Historical and Archaeological Society have been particularly helpful, both in terms of encouragement offered and information provided. In particular, sincere thanks go to David Picken for many helpful suggestions, and for taking many of the present-day photographs in the book. The staff at Aldershot Library all deserve special thanks, for without their forbearance and understanding the writing of this book would have been many times more difficult.

Our sincerest thanks go to the following individuals and organisations for the loan of photographs and illustrations and for the permission to use them in the book: Aldershot Library (Hampshire County Council), 1-3, 6-9, 11, 14-17, 22, 24, 26-36, 38-65, 67-76, 78-82, 85-104, 107-10, 112, 115-19, 121-46; Mrs. Sally Lawrence, 66 and 113; Miss M. Collier, 77; Mrs. Janet Bragg *née* Edmunds, 83 and 84; Mr. Eric Clifford, 105-6; Mrs. Alice Phillips, 111; Mr. Ray Biles, 114. All the remaining illustrations were provided by the authors.

Our special thanks go to Mr. Ian Maine of the Aldershot Military Museum for being ever ready to help, both in terms of suggestions and in the loan of materials; his support was most valuable and much appreciated.

If we have inadvertently omitted to thank anyone, we do give our most sincere apologies.

Chapter One

The Village of Aldershott

Most towns the size of present-day Aldershot can trace their history back through the years, perhaps to a mention in William the Conqueror's Domesday Book, or to a settlement founded by the Romans. In some respects Aldershot is no different, for its history can be followed for well over a thousand years, yet the town has experienced no prolonged period of steady growth with its size increasing inexorably from one decade to the next. For the first 970 years of its recorded existence, before the arrival of the Army, Aldershot remained a small and unimportant village, almost entirely ignored by weighty events taking place on the national and international stage. It was fairly typical of hundreds—thousands even—of villages scattered across the country. Its population was small, and did not even number 500 until the early 1800s, yet from time to time Aldershot does emerge from obscurity to give us a clue as to what the place was like.

Long before written records began to be kept there is evidence of human activity in the area. The two best examples of this are the prehistoric earthworks known as Caesar's Camp

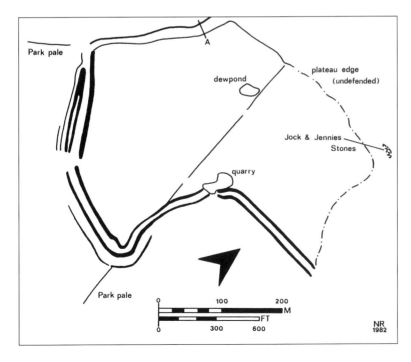

1 Caesar's Camp was constructed in the Iron Age as a tribal defensive outpost. The 'park pale' refers to the boundary of a medieval deer park.

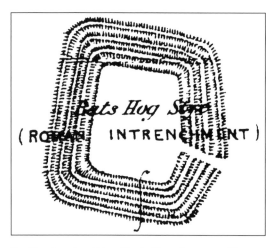

2   Despite describing Batt's Hog Stye as a 'Roman Intrenchment', it was probably the site of an early Celtic chieftain's homestead. This plan is on a scale of approximately 56 inches to the mile, and is taken from the Ordnance Survey map of 1855.

and Batt's Hog Stye, situated on Bricksbury Hill and in Claycart Bottom respectively. The name 'Caesar's Camp' is a definite misnomer as the earthworks date from the Iron Age with the best guess for the date of their construction being around 300 B.C.; the name of 'Caesar's Camp' was only applied to the site in the 18th century. The purpose of the 'Camp' was most likely as a defensive fortification, and by the time of the Roman invasion of Britain it had become an outpost of the region occupied by the Belgae, an early British tribe whose area of dominance extended from the Channel to the Aldershot area and beyond. The 'Camp' itself is a large, irregularly-shaped construction, which makes good use of the natural contours of the site, and would have been one of a number of such fortifications on the frontiers of tribal territories. Batt's Hog Stye is of later date and one theory for its function is that it was the homestead of an early Celtic Chieftain. It is nearly square in shape, having rounded corners and measuring 50 yards by 56 yards. It is surrounded by four earth ramparts and three ditches. These have been much eroded by the passage of time, the

ramparts only rising 18 inches above the level of the surrounding ground with the ditches of similar depth below ground level.

The earliest recorded mention of Aldershot occurs in King Alfred's will dating from the early 880s, in which he left the Hundred of Crondall to his nephew, Ethelm, the village of Aldershot forming part of this bequest. Nearly a hundred years then pass before Aldershot again creeps into view, when in 975 King Edgar granted the Hundred to the monastery of Winchester Cathedral 'for the support of the monks dwelling therein'. Amongst the manuscripts from the Winchester Cathedral library is a record of the feudal customs, services and payments from the holders of lands in the 24 manors belonging to the Prior and Convent of St Swithun (which included the manor of Crondall). The manuscript dates from the middle of the 14th century, some time after 1325, and lists 'Alresshate'.

After the reformation of 1541 it appears that the tenures and customs of the Manor of Crondall had drifted into a state of confusion and uncertainty. In 1567, during the reign of Queen Elizabeth I, the Dean and Chapter of Winchester drew up a new Customary for the manor. One copy of this indenture was for many years in the possession of the Parish of Aldershot, where it was kept securely locked in a large chest in the belfry of St Michael's Church. More recently, it was for many years on display in the Local History Room of Aldershot Library, but it is now in the County Record Office in Winchester. Several field and place names mentioned in 'The Tithing of Alrisshott' in the Crondall Customary such as Ashebridge, Birchettes, Cranmoor Lane, Dudbrook, Hiegate, West end and Tongehambridge are recognisable today. During the Civil War in the mid-17th century the cathedral lands were seized by Parliament, but on the Restoration of Charles II the *status quo* was restored and the land remained in the ownership of the Dean and Chapter of Winchester until 1861, when it was vested in the

Ecclesiastical Commission in common with other church property.

The parish church itself, dedicated to St Michael, dates from the 12th century, although it has since been much enlarged and restored. The church was pre-dated by an even earlier building, as records exist which refer to an 11th-century chapel at Aldershot. That other mainstay of village life, the manor house, has a history stretching back at least as far as 1481, when the house was sold by one John Awbery of Aldershot to a triumvirate consisting of Richard Newbrigge, the vicar of Farnham, John Brown, Clerk to the King's Chancellery and to Richard Balche, a cloth maker also of Farnham. The present building dates from 1670 and replaced the original building, traces of which remained on the site of Aldershot Park until the bathing pools complex was built in the 1920s. The manor had been in possession of the White and Tichborne families for nearly two hundred years from the early 1500s, and both these inter-related families are commemorated in the parish church.

3 The rear of the Manor House in a photograph taken just before the Second World War. The tall tree on the right was a 100-year-old magnolia tree, cut down when the Heroes' Shrine was built.

4 The Manor House was built in 1670 by the Tichborne family and replaced a much earlier building which had fallen into disrepair.

A few years after the construction of the present Manor House an event took place in Aldershot—or perhaps more accurately, is alleged to have taken place—which, had things turned out differently, may well have created some impression on the national stage. The story goes that in February 1675, Nell Gwynn, King Charles II's mistress, was travelling from Portsmouth to London, when signs of distress and tiredness overcame her. As the weather was wet and dark, shelter was sought in the *Fox and Hounds* inn, which still survives today, just inside the county boundary on Weybourne

Road, although now converted to residential use. A servant was dispatched to find a local surgeon, but only the village midwife, Mother Squalls, was to be found; the nature of Nell Gwynn's distress soon became clear, and later that evening a male child was born dead, perhaps due to the absence of more sophisticated medical knowledge than Mother Squalls was able to provide. The body was taken away by Jem May, Mother Squalls' son, and by Master Vernon, the son of the local landowner who lived at Aldershot Park Mansion, and was buried near a yew tree in St Michael's churchyard in conditions of the strictest secrecy. Vernon then rode to London to inform the king of what had happened, and after five days Nell Gwynn's party resumed their journey to London, with the secret still intact.

A little over one hundred years after this story occurs the first military connection with Aldershot. In 1792 a temporary camp was established on Beacon Hill for troops taking part in manoeuvres in the area, and it is tempting to speculate that some recollection of the success of this exercise lingered in the governmental memory when the decision was taken more than sixty years later to establish the permanent camp at Aldershot.

It is difficult now to visualise the kind of place Aldershot must have been prior to the arrival of the Army in the 1850s. Its population was increasing slowly in the first half of the 19th century; in 1801 there were 494 inhabitants, in 1841 there were 685, and in 1851, the year of the last census before the arrival of the Army, there were 875. The census of 1851 may therefore provide a typical picture of the people of Aldershot as they were before the coming of the camp, as the only changes between 1851 and 1854 would have been the normal births, marriages, deaths, emigrations and immigrations. The main occupation of these inhabitants was agriculture, indeed nearly a

5 The former *Fox and Hounds* inn on Weybourne Road. Legend has it that King Charles II's mistress Nell Gwynn gave birth to an illegitimate baby here in 1675.

hundred of the male population of 438 described themselves as 'agricultural labourers', and a further 16 as 'farmers'. This was in common with the majority of the population of Victorian England whose lifestyle pre-1851 was rural, not urban. The village of Aldershot was self-sufficient, with a baker, butcher, grocer, blacksmith, wheelwright, veterinary surgeon and three carpenters. The inhabitants would have been spread over a fairly wide area, with the largest cluster of houses centred around the village green, which still survives today as a triangle of grass at the junction of High Street and Church Hill. There were two inns, the *Red Lion*, where the innkeeper was also a plumber, and the *Beehive*, both of which exist today in rebuilt premises.

The gentry were represented by the occupants of the two 'big' houses. Captain George Newcome (one of six ex-military men living in the village), his wife and five servants lived at the Manor House in Manor Park, and Charles Barron and five servants lived in Aldershott Place. (The present spelling of 'Aldershot' only became generally accepted in about 1860; the name itself means a copse of alder trees.) The only church, St Michael's, was served by a curate, the Rev. Henry Carey, although the Rev. Arthur Bradley, a single man

described as 'a clergyman M.A.', lodged elsewhere. In the religious census of 1851, Henry Carey reported that the church held a total of 270 people, and that 244 attended morning service and 309 (!) attended evening service on census day, Sunday 30 March. Thomas Attfield was the parish clerk.

There was little industry in the village, some potters and brickmakers, a tile maker, a brick burner (whose wife was a ladies' corset maker), and a retired glazier and house painter. Most of these would be involved in selling their skills to the local population. There is a local bed of clay from which coarse common pottery ware has been made, similar to that produced at Cove, where peat fuel was dug close at hand for its manufacture. There was a school which stood at what is now Hospital Hill. The Union School was for the poorer children of the surrounding area of the county and had 100 scholars who thus formed a large part of the 875 inhabitants of Aldershot. In the early years of the 19th century this building— still standing today—had been used as the local workhouse, and before that, had been the manor house of the Tichborne family, replacing a dilapidated earlier version situated in Aldershot Park. By 1808, however, the building was being used as a workhouse, which also owned

6 An engraving made in 1856 of St Michael's parish church, showing how it looked before later alterations were made.

7 & 8   The front and rear of Aldershot Park mansion. The house was built in 1842 by Charles Barron, but was demolished in the 1960s to make way for Place Court old people's home.

9 Church Hill pictured in the 1930s. This area would have been the focal point of 'Aldershott' village with Manor Park to the right and the parish church and the Manor House itself situated further up the hill. The grassy area in the foreground is all that remains of the old village green.

four fields as part of its land. During the 1830s and 1840s the provision of relief to the poor was an issue affecting parishes across the land, and Aldershot was no exception. In 1836 the rate was fixed at 1s. 3d. in the pound for the relief and maintenance of the poor, although this was later raised to 1s. 8d. The sums thus raised were used in a variety of ways to alleviate the ravages of poverty, most often in allowing the recipient of alms to purchase food, or sometimes to obtain medical treatment, if necessary. In 1843 Thomas Smith was appointed Assistant Overseer on a salary of £26 per annum. Four years later, it was decided to incorporate the Aldershot workhouse into the Farnham Union, and it was at this point that the building was first used as the pauper school. The building

itself undoubtedly incorporates much material from the Tichborne manor house of 1680, although it is questionable how much remains structurally from that date. It has certainly been altered at various times in its history and to complicate matters still further, a fire in 1907 caused extensive damage to the property, necessitating a certain amount of rebuilding work as a result.

The surrounding countryside would have been mostly heathland, almost treeless in nature, and crossed by only a few tracks. The nearest road was the ancient trackway along the Hog's Back, which by now was a turnpike road linking London to Portsmouth via Guildford and Farnham; along this road lay a system of semaphore towers for communication between the War Office and the important naval base at Portsmouth. There was a semaphore signal at Tongham near where the *Hog's Back Hotel* now stands. There was also a turnpike road through Farnborough where stagecoaches ran.

Other forms of transport in the area included the Basingstoke Canal, built to link the agricultural and food-producing areas of north Hampshire with potential markets in London. The construction of the canal entailed the arrival of teams of navvies in October 1788 and had a great impact on the Aldershot area. Using the only tools available in the 18th century—picks and shovels—they commenced the great engineering work, the construction of a long, curving embankment stretching from beyond the wharf at Ash to the only lock in Hampshire at Aldershot, over the low-lying ground through which the River Blackwater flowed. From Aldershot Lock the canal was dug at the same level for 21 miles to its terminus at Basingstoke. The route lay through the great heath between Aldershot and Fleet. The embankment was built using the spoil from the thousand-yard cutting, in places 70 ft. deep, which came to be known as Deepcut, near Pirbright, where a set of 14 locks within two miles was constructed. The census of 1851 lists inhabitants in Aldershot with the occupation of lock keeper and wharfinger, reflecting the influence the canal had along the length of its course.

The main London & South Western Railway (LSWR) was built in the early 1840s to Southampton, enabling produce to be carried from the local station at Farnborough. In 1849 a branch line was opened from Guildford to Farnham, and three years later was extended to Alton, with the intention of carrying hops and locally brewed beer. The stations nearest to Aldershot were at Tongham and Ash Green.

The local market towns were Farnham and Guildford in Surrey, and Alton and Basingstoke in Hampshire.

Aldershot was thus a windswept, remote little village, well off the beaten track, and unknown to all but those with local connections. When the announcement was first made in the London newspapers that the area around the village of Aldershot had been bought for the purpose of constructing a military camp, many correspondents were forced to enquire where Aldershot was, such was the obscurity of the location. The town to which the area looked as its natural centre was Farnham, but prior to 1854 the only way to reach Aldershot from there was to walk or go on horseback along roads which today we would consider as little more than farm tracks. Before the Farnborough Road—now the A325—was built, the main route from Farnham to Farnborough ran through Badshot Lea, along Lower Farnham Road and North Lane, then through Aldershot Stubs, along Hollybush Lane and on to Sycamore Road.

The buildings of the village would have been few and fairly well scattered, with pathways linking the main collections of dwellings to the focal points of the village, such as the church, the two pubs and the few shops that existed. Apart from cottages and other buildings in the vicinity of Manor Park, there were no houses on the north side of High Street and the Union School mentioned earlier would have been nearly a mile from the main centre of the village, such as it was at that time. All this was about to change in a way that was probably far beyond the imagination of most of Aldershot's 875 inhabitants, when the first small party of Royal Engineers arrived in 1853 to set up camp on what is now the Prince's Gardens.

Chapter Two

The Army Arrive

The decision to establish a permanent military camp had been some years in the making; before the Army settled upon Aldershot as their new 'home', barracks had been concentrated in ancient forts or castles situated in towns and cities which afforded little or no scope for engaging in larger-scale military manoeuvres. Such exercises had, in fact, taken place in earlier years, but on land which had been rented by the Army specifically for the purpose, and which after the manoeuvres had finished, reverted to something like its original use. Lord Hardinge, the Commander-in-Chief of the Army, with the not inconsiderable support of Prince Albert, the Prince Consort, now realised that a permanent home for the Army was of the utmost importance. Not only had Great Britain a fast-growing Empire to look after, but across the English Channel in France, Louis Napoleon Bonaparte, nephew of the great Napoleon defeated at Waterloo, had had himself proclaimed Emperor Napoleon III in 1852. Although this new Napoleon was soon to show that he was but a pale imitation of his uncle, the name of Bonaparte still cast an uncomfortably long shadow over British military thinking; in 1852, Waterloo was still a recent memory.

So why was Aldershot chosen, rather than other, more suitable locations? The answer, perhaps, is simply that Aldershot *was* the most suitable location. It was situated approximately half-way between London and the great naval port of Portsmouth; there were rail links close

at hand which facilitated the rapid transport of troops and equipment; the area was heathland, not given over to agriculture in the way that other areas were; and finally, there was a plentiful natural supply of water which was lacking in some of the other locations under consideration, the most notable of which was the area around Reigate. There was, however, a need for some urgency in the purchase of the land. Similar areas were rapidly being enclosed and in many cases turned over to agricultural use, which would have made the acquisition of the land a much more difficult procedure. Consequently, on 11 January 1854 an agreement was reached with the owners of Aldershot Heath that the land would be purchased at £12 an acre. A sum of £100,000 was included in the Army Estimates, although in the course of the next seven years this figure would rise to nearly £150,000, involving the purchase of nearly 8,000 acres of land.

Little more than a month later work began on building the camp, with the first of some 1,200 wooden huts being erected in what is now North Camp, at a cost of £150 each. However, events elsewhere resulted in the new camp developing in a very different way from the original plans. On 28 March 1854, war was declared against Russia, and such was the popularity of the war that many influential figures, not least of whom was the Prince Consort, wasted no time in urging that the camp be constructed with more permanent buildings, thus ensuring the long-term future of Aldershot as

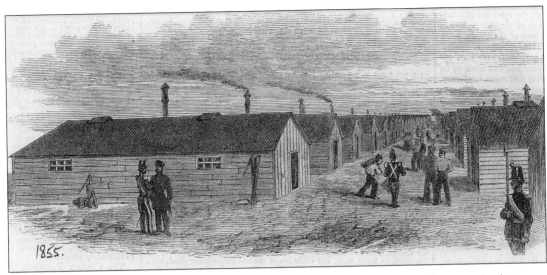

10   An early depiction from 1855 of the 'temporary' wooden huts in South Camp. These wooden huts were among the first buildings erected by the Army in Aldershot.

11   'O' lines pictured nearly forty years later in a scene which could almost be that of the earlier drawing. The huts were found still to be in good condition when they were demolished in the 1890s.

12 A view of the Basingstoke Canal from about 1914 as it passes under the Farnborough Road. The canal had been built in the last years of the 18th century and it was at this location that much of the building material for the camp was unloaded.

the primary base of the British Army. As a result, in September 1854 work began on the building of the permanent barracks, the first phase of which was completed in 1859. Construction of the wooden 'temporary' huts continued alongside, although it should perhaps be mentioned that when the last of these huts were demolished 40 years later, they were found still to be in excellent condition!

The building of the camp at Aldershot meant that fortune smiled on the Basingstoke Canal for perhaps the first and only time in its entire history. It had never been a prosperous waterway or a great commercial success. At first, the increase in trade was small—the only additional barge traffic to Aldershot in 1854 was the carriage of 22 tons of fencing from London and 78 tons of earthenware pipes from

Reading. However, by 1855 the principal cargoes were timber and deal boarding for the huts, bricks for the foundations, roofing slates, paving stones, iron pipes and tar. As huts for 12,000 men were to be built on the south side of the canal and huts for 8,000 on the north side, there was need for a method of communication between the two camps, and in September 1855 an eight-ton pontoon bridge was built on the site of the present-day bridge on Queen's Avenue. Within the space of three years 20,000 tons of building materials and commodities had been brought by water to the new camp. Each barge had carried on average a cargo of over 40 tons, sometimes as much as 60 tons, so that a return cargo from Aldershot was not essential for profitable performance.

13   A scene from 1855 showing building materials being unloaded for the camp at the Basingstoke Canal. The location is just south of the canal on the Farnborough Road. The building on the right is the *Row Barge Inn* and a room was let to the Royal Engineers during the construction of the camp; later General Knollys used it as a temporary headquarters. Somewhat ungratefully, the Army ordered its demolition in 1859, deciding the inn had served its purpose.

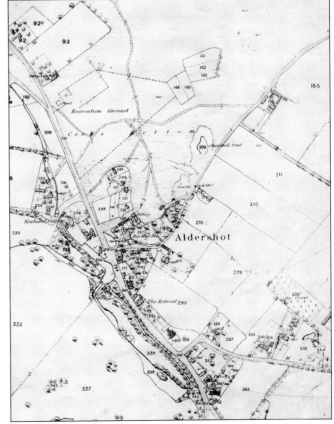

14   A map on the scale of 25 inches to the mile, dated 1855, showing the layout of the village of Aldershot, as yet very little altered by the arrival of the Army.

The *Row Barge Inn* by Farnham Road Wharf was one of the original inns of Aldershot. Until the coming of the camp it had only catered for bargees and travellers on the turnpike road to Winchester; now it did a roaring trade, and the innkeeper, James Houghton let out a room for the use of the Engineers' Department. The inn later became the temporary headquarters of the general and his staff and meals were obtainable for his officers. On the completion of the camp, the army authorities decided that the inn, which was now on government land, and which had acquired a dubious reputation through being frequented by ladies of easy virtue, should be closed down. Houghton was served with six months notice to quit, but he did not act upon his eviction until a party of sappers began dismantling the inn by removing its roof.

The first troops had arrived in early May, and they were followed by vast numbers of other soldiers throughout the summer, many of whom were in effect only 'passing through' before being sent to the Crimea via the naval base at Portsmouth. In addition to the red-coated Army *en route* for Russia, another army of labourers was descending on Aldershot to assist in the building of the new barracks. Attracted by the high wages on offer, this new army were accommodated in a kind of shanty

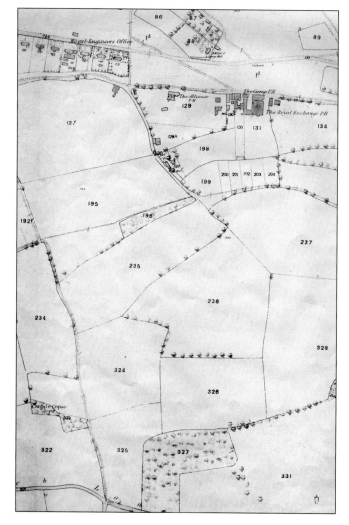

15 Another section of the 1855 map, showing the area of what is now High Street from the Prince's Gardens to the Recreation Ground. Already no fewer than three public houses are shown, and it is interesting to note that the movement has begun of the centre of Aldershot from the old village to a site approximately 600 yards away.

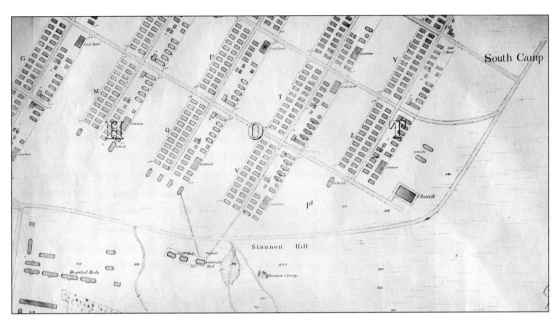

16 The rows of the 'temporary' huts are clearly visible, immediately to the north of the opposite map. The field system, clearly shown near the old village, is conspicuous by its absence in the land newly acquired by the Army.

town which quickly sprang up on the edges of the camp; High Street in Aldershot and Lynchford Road in North Camp are the direct descendants of these early commercial efforts. Wages drawn by the workmen were sometimes five times what they had been earning—as agricultural labourers perhaps—in civilian life, and for many of them so much money was burning a very large hole in their pockets.

Inevitably, many of the entertainments were fuelled by alcohol and sex, both of which were readily and cheaply available. Many of the drinking dens had a back 'room' in which distinctly downmarket music hall acts would appear, doubtless to the accompaniment of enthusiastic if drunken applause. Elsewhere, in hastily erected tents, prostitutes would entertain their clients, or if their resources would not stretch to a tent, anywhere outside where a degree of privacy could be guaranteed. Perhaps unsurprisingly, this period marked a huge increase in cases of syphilis and illegitimacy in the surrounding area, but these were not the

only problems facing the erstwhile village. The provision of sanitary arrangements in this township was notable by its absence, with the result that household and personal waste were at best simply buried in the ground, or at worst, just dumped wherever one pleased. The stench of such waste quickly became unbearable and, if they could afford it, many of the workmen left to seek lodgings in nearby Farnham. Many visitors and residents succumbed to diseases born of the insanitary conditions and Aldershot at this juncture must have truly resembled a gold rush town of the Klondike or of some other frontier post far from the centre of civilisation.

Nevertheless, work continued apace on the construction of the camp and of the civilian town which was springing up around it. In April 1855, Lt.-General Sir William Knollys was appointed General Officer commanding the camp, and with the support of the Prince Consort he energetically set about improving the organisation of the troops, while not being above sharing some of their hardships under canvas. In the same month the site was selected for the Royal Pavilion, which was intended to be a temporary residence for Queen Victoria whilst she visited the troops at Aldershot. Both the site and design were chosen by the Prince Consort, the former being selected during a visit on 2 April, when the Prince insisted that the boundaries of the site be marked out before he left. The Queen paid her first visit to Aldershot in June 1855, on which occasion tea was taken in the Pavilion, although the building was not fit for overnight residency at this stage. It was not until the following April that the Queen first stayed in the Royal Pavilion to mark the formal completion of the camp. On this occasion she inspected the 14,000 troops then stationed at Aldershot, after which she and the Prince Consort stayed the night in the newly completed Royal residence.

The end of the Crimean War in March 1856 meant that large numbers of troops were now returning to Britain, and in particular to Aldershot. Accommodating these men during the warm summer months presented no great problems, but with the onset of winter the situation began to deteriorate, causing HRH The Duke of Cambridge to write to the Secretary of State for War, Lord Panmure in order to draw the matter to his attention. It was probably the Duke's letter which did much to seal the future of Aldershot as a permanent camp and garrison along the lines which were to exist for many years to come. Two trophies of the Crimean War deserve a mention here. The first of these is the Sebastopol Bell, which was one of a pair, the other residing in Windsor Castle. Originally sited outside the Headquarters Offices on Middle Hill, the bell was struck

17   The Royal Pavilion was built for Queen Victoria and was originally known as the Queen's Pavilion. Situated on the western side of Farnborough Road, it was demolished in the early 1960s.

18   *Right.* An interior view of the Royal Pavilion in the late 1850s.

19   *Below.* The Headquarters of the Camp in the 1850s. The Royal Pavilion can just be seen in the background.

20   *Bottom.* Showing one of Queen Victoria's first visits to the Camp, this print of 1855 gives a good impression of the bleakness of the surrounding heathland, and of the large expanse of countryside available to the military.

every hour by a sentry, before it was removed and re-hung in the bell tower of the newly built Cambridge Military Hospital in 1879. The second trophy was the Time Gun, which resided at the top of Gun Hill until the Hospital was built, when it was removed to a site outside the Military Cemetery. Until the First World War it had been fired every day at one o'clock as a time signal, and at half past nine in the evening as a warning to troops to return to their quarters.

It was in about 1856 that Aldershot's first railway was constructed. Hitherto, the nearest railway station was at Tongham, from where

materials had to be carried slowly and laboriously by horse and cart along bumpy, badly surfaced roads. Accordingly, a light railway was built from Tongham which crossed the Ash Road just east of the *Greyhound Inn* before crossing North Lane at its northernmost end and then running parallel to High Street nearly as far as the Farnborough Road. It was not to be until 1870 that Aldershot would acquire its own railway station.

As the barracks grew, so did the other facilities available to the troops. One of these was the Prince Consort's Library, which opened in 1860. As its name implies, it was supported

21   Prior to the construction of the military narrow gauge railway, all building materials had to be transported the last few miles to the barracks over bumpy, unreliable roads. This light railway connected the building sites to Tongham railway station.

22   The Prince Consort's Library pictured in about 1890 before the addition of the Lecture Hall and Reading Room extension. Prince Albert provided much of the necessary funding for the library from his own private resources and had been purchasing books for it from as early as 1857.

23 'The Royal Aldershott Club House' was built in 1859 on what is now the site of *Potter's International Hotel.* It was built at the instigation of a London wine merchant, and the Prince Consort became its first patron.

by Prince Albert, in common with many of the other early initiatives connected with the building of the camp. The cost of the building was met by the Prince himself, and when the library opened in October 1860, many of the 1,200 volumes on the shelves had also been provided by the Prince, who had been buying books since 1857 with the library very much in mind. For those minded to follow less intellectual pursuits there was little on offer apart from the drinking dens and bawdy houses already mentioned. There were, however, early attempts at establishing amateur theatre within the camp. A large hut, with a seating capacity of 500, which opened in April 1856, provided the venue for the camp's first theatre. Queen Victoria even attended a performance there later that year, after which it was known as The Theatre Royal, not to be confused with a later theatre of the same name in civilian Aldershot. An Aldershot Musical Society was formed at about the same time, and several 'creditable' concerts were produced. Visiting choirs from London also appeared from time to time, so the entertainments were by no means limited exclusively to those of the theatrical kind.

The spiritual welfare of the troops was not neglected, either. No fewer than three churches were built; all of which were constructed out of wood and iron. One was even known as the 'Iron Church' and was situated just to the north of the Recreation Ground until it was moved in 1866 to the site now occupied by St Andrew's Church on Queen's Avenue. Another was the Roman Catholic Church of St Michael and St Sebastian, which stood near the Cambridge Military Hospital, while the third church stood in Evelyn Woods Road in North Camp. It was in 1858 that the Officers' Club was first built on the Farnborough Road. This was done on the initiative of Thomas Stapleton, a London wine merchant, with the backing of Lt.-General Knollys. Almost inevitably, the Prince Consort took a major interest in the project, and agreed to become patron of the club. The premises included a reading room, a coffee room, a card room, a fencing room, a smoking room, and three billiards rooms, amongst others.

The following year, Aldershot gained its first newspaper, the *Aldershot Military Gazette and General Advertiser,* the first issue of which appeared on Saturday, 6 August 1859. Although undergoing more than one change of name, this newspaper appeared weekly until after the First World War, and provided a valuable

24 The Officers' Club in about 1958. Having undergone a major rebuilding programme in the 1930s, it bears little resemblance to the original building.

commentary on the events taking place in both the military camp and the civilian town. This first issue, costing one penny, contained (amongst other things) advertisements for no less than six inns or hotels, four ironmongers, four cobblers and three bakers. There were also two undertakers, one of whom, Finch's, is still in existence today, and on the front page alone, there were also advertisements for a butcher, a baker and a candlestick maker! Three years later the Army gymnasium was built. This had the distinction of being not only the first Army gymnasium in Aldershot, but also the first to be built by the British Army anywhere. This followed a directive from the War Office that the training of the troops should include not merely drill and weapons training, but also address the general physical fitness of the soldier.

In many respects, the year 1861 was a turning point in the story of military Aldershot. At the end of the year, Prince Albert the

Prince Consort died at the early age of 42 after contracting typhoid fever from the unhygienic and antiquated drains at Windsor Castle. Without his vision and drive it is very likely that the Aldershot of today, or even of 1861 would have been a very different place indeed. By 1861 the first phase in the construction of the camp and town had passed—not that the cycle of building, demolition and rebuilding has ever really ended—and Aldershot could look forward towards consolidating its position as a growing town in its own right. It is also a useful point at which to pause for a moment and reflect upon the mighty changes which had taken place since the arrival of the Army seven years earlier.

The 1851 census had shown a village predominantly dependent on agriculture. Ten years on, the 1861 census showed a very different picture as the rural village of Aldershot had transmogrified into a burgeoning

Victorian town whose inhabitants were mainly young. They were incomers not just from the surrounding areas of Hampshire, Surrey and Berkshire, but from the whole of the south of England and from the Midlands, Scotland, Ireland and Wales, all drawn to a rapidly expanding growth area. The civilian population of the town numbered nearly 5,000, and was evenly divided between male and female. The number of agricultural labourers and those engaged in rural occupations had fallen to less than 90; indeed, the most popular civilian employment in Aldershot was that of boot maker or of publican. There was a large number of public houses, inns, hotels and beer houses in the town, and their names reflected their clientele, ranging from those with militaristic titles such as *Indian Hero, Wellington Arms, Military Hotel* and *Imperial Hussars* to the more general *White Hart, Rising Sun, Fox and Hounds, Royal Standard* or the more specialised *Brickmaker's Delight*. Nearly fifty of the male population list their occupation as that of inn-

keeper, hotel keeper, publican, beer house keeper or beer seller, and sometimes this occupation was combined with another, as in the landlord of the *Duke of York,* who was also a blacksmith, and William Haslett of the *White Hart* in Cambridge Terrace who was described as 'beer house keeper and builder'.

Many of the public houses offered 'entertainment' and there were many musicians, vocalists and comedians listed as part of their staff. Other entertainers lodged elsewhere in the town. Five professional musicians and a bandmaster lived in Church Lane; in Union Street lodged Walter Harris from Portsmouth, a comic singer, and Joseph Atkins, a clog dancer from Shoreditch, London. In the same street two of the lodgers of Walter Alcock, a pastry cook, were Edwin Martin, aged 23, a 'delineator of Negro life' (a now politically incorrect blacked up minstrel) and Henry Conway, aged 21, a 'dancer and comic singer'. Benjamin Bodell, an actor from Chelsea, and Thomas and Dulcibella Lawrence, a comedian

25   Aldershot Market taken from a print of 1859. In a very short space of time Aldershot acquired many of the facilities expected in a fair-sized town.

and actress, lived in nearby Havelock Street. Grace Alleyne, a vocalist from London, also lived nearby. Lower down the social scale an unnamed fiddler from Gloucester, his wife and three children lived 'not in a house', but presumably in a gypsy caravan.

There is only one prostitute named on the census and she is a 20-year-old from Lancashire who was a prisoner in the police cells on the night of the census (7 April 1861), together with five others whose occupations are listed as a soldier, a tramp, a labourer, a cordwainer and a thief, possibly a typical cross-section of the town's criminal population. There are two unmarried females elsewhere in the town who intriguingly list their occupation as 'professional', whilst various lodging houses have a high occupancy of females between the ages of 16 and 28 whose occupation is 'nil'. Respectable females on the census mostly have a blank space where the occupation is listed, so maybe the enumerator is trying to tell the reader something with typical Victorian reticence!

Some of the familiar business names in Aldershot make their first appearance on this census. Thomas White, a 48-year-old draper and outfitter, has an establishment in High Street and employs two clerks, two porters, two apprentices, two milliners, a clothier, an outfitter and 15 drapers (eight female and seven male), all of whom live on the premises, and who are attended by four domestic servants. Further down the street, Moses Phillips from Poland had set up in business as a pawnbroker and jeweller, whilst nearby, Woolf Cohen, another immigrant from Russia (with a Polish wife), is a Marine Stores Dealer. Also in High Street, Henry Allen combines his business in the Post Office with that of a chemist and druggist. In North Lane, 34-year-old William Bartram from Melbourne in Derbyshire has opened a business as a horse slaughterer, reminding us of the Victorian dependence on horse power both for civilian and military purposes. In the days before the railway reached Aldershot, on the banks of the Basingstoke

Canal at Aldershot Wharf, were a carrier business employing seven carters, Charles Hill, a boat proprietor, and William Burle, a wharfinger and coal merchant.

Many of the soldiers' wives found lodgings around the perimeter of the camp, swelling the number of the population. Some Army officers also dwelt in the town and maintained a complement of servants befitting their rank and style. Because of the newness of the town there was no recognised upper class area. For example, in Cranmore Lane an agricultural labourer and his family lived near to two military families, a Captain in the 45th Regiment, his family and four servants, and a Captain in the Royal Hussars, his family and five servants. There is one 'Chelsea Pensioner', a lone representative of retired soldiery, listed on the census. There were extremes of poverty and respectability in Aldershot. The enumerator noted that 'two persons had left home on the night of 7 April' from Union Street (in order to avoid him, maybe?). Nearby dwelt an 'old clothes dealer' from Ireland. Respectability and the emerging middle classes were represented by the presence in the town of a bank manager, a surgeon, a dentist, three lawyers, three Professors of Music, a Professor of Chemistry and a Professor of Gymnastics, whilst law and order were maintained by the presence of a Police Superintendent, four Police Constables and their families.

Finally, two examples of a 'local boy made good' and of the change from an agricultural economy to an urban one: in Cavendish Villas lived John Martin from Hartley Row, Hampshire, who was a 40-year-old builder employing 100 men and four boys. In Cranmore Lane an agricultural labourer had one son who had followed his father's profession. His younger son was employed as a labourer in a brickfield, and probably earned more than either his father or his elder brother. Also in the household lodged a bricklayer, a sign of things to come with the development of the town and camp.

Chapter Three

The Growth of the Town

As the 1850s gave way to the 1860s, the fledgling town slowly began to gather about itself the trappings of municipal organisation. These first steps towards the regulation of its own affairs were at first haphazard in nature, little more than a reaction to the rapidly moving events taking place in north-east Hampshire. In fact, the first stirrings of civic pride had occurred in November 1857 when the first meeting of the local Board of Health was held, the result of a petition to Parliament for the Public Health Act of 1854 to be made applicable to Aldershot. The board was composed of several prominent local residents, although the Army was not represented until later when three officers, including General Knollys, the General Officer Commanding the Camp, were added to the board. The first meeting of this expanded committee was held on 6 April 1858, and can be seen as the first attempt to stem the tide of insanitary conditions that were rife in the newly founded town.

In November 1860, three years after the establishment of the Board of Health, the Aldershot Burial Board met for the first time. This body's deliberations resulted in the opening of a cemetery at the bottom of Redan Hill, and two chapels were later erected, one catering for Church of England customers, the other for those of Nonconformist persuasion. Four years after the initial opening of the cemetery, the Jewish Community approached the Burial Board and asked if they might purchase a portion of the land to be used for burials for members of their faith. This was duly agreed, and permission was sought from, and granted by, the Home Secretary, Sir George Grey. It is interesting to note that a temporary Jewish Synagogue had been in existence since as early as 1858, with sufficient strength of numbers by 1864 to warrant the making of this request.

As the town grew in size, so the Public Utilities correspondingly grew in importance. The Aldershot Gas and Water Company was formed in 1866, replacing an earlier concern and greatly expanding its operations at the same time. But perhaps Aldershot's most obvious need at this time was for improved communications with the outside world, not least of all London itself, and Portsmouth, the potential point of embarkation for any overseas military expedition. At this point, it should perhaps be recalled that the only way to transport large numbers of troops or large amounts of building material was by rail, and the nearest railway station to Aldershot was some two or three miles away as the crow flies, at Tongham, and considerably further on the ground, allowing for the circuitous course of the local roads. Accordingly, work began on building a line through Pirbright to Aldershot and on to Farnham, which opened in May 1870. The railway station, opened in the same year, at that time stood in open fields, the nearest buildings being perhaps half a mile away in Victoria Road or High Street.

26 Aldershot Military Cemetery pictured in about 1910 with the railway line in the background and, beyond that, the Basingstoke Canal.

27 Aldershot Railway Station pictured in about 1903. The scene has changed remarkably little today, although, when the station was built in 1870, it was situated in open fields.

By now, nearly twenty years had passed since the first arrival of the Army and a degree of Victorian respectability had settled on the rapidly developing town. One of the earliest manifestations of this was the establishment of the Mission Hall, founded by Louisa Daniell in 1862. Mrs. Daniell was the widow of a military captain who had been invited to Aldershot by a male member of an organisation called the Country Towns Mission. He had been appalled by the immoral and insanitary conditions in the town, which gravely threatened the health and welfare of the troops. Mrs. Daniell was a woman of earnest piety, holding strong Protestant views and, perhaps with this in mind, he wrote to her, asking her to 'adopt' Aldershot. Whilst staying in a Midlands village recuperating after illness, she became convinced that many poor country folk were neglected by the established church and were thus in need of conversion and salvation. She had started evangelical missions to improve the moral, spiritual and material welfare of thousands of common country folk and her missionary work was well known to the Country Towns Mission.

Upon her arrival in the town, Mrs. Daniell leased a house as a temporary Mission Hall and reading room. She liaised with those sections of the military personnel who disassociated themselves from the immorality of the town, and who attempted to follow Christian ideals. With their help and co-operation the Mission Hall grew in popularity with the troops and was an immediate success. Hundreds of young men forsook the drinking and vice dens of the town to frequent the Hall, where they could drink nothing stronger than tea or coffee (no alcohol was allowed), eat, read and partake in prayer meetings and hymn singing.

The establishment soon outgrew its premises, and in 1863 the Earl of Shaftesbury, the prominent Christian and social reformer, laid the foundation stone of what he officially named the Soldiers' Home and Institute on a site in Barrack Road, donated to Mrs. Daniell

by a well-wisher. The new home was opened on Sunday, 11 October 1865 to a week of continuous rejoicing and prayer. She was assisted in her mission work by her devoted spinster daughter Georgina Daniell, who had accompanied her mother to Aldershot and continued working in the Institute for 23 years after her mother's death in 1871. During this time the Aldershot Institute was greatly enlarged, and other branches were established for the troops and sailors in Colchester, Plymouth, Chatham, Windsor, London and Okehampton. In Portsmouth, Agnes Weston used a disused music hall as a 'sailors' rest' in 1870, and Sarah Robinson opened a Soldiers' Institute in 1874. Sarah condemned the Portsmouth prostitutes in 1890 as being 'bolder than anywhere else, older, uglier and more experienced', and claimed that she had seen and heard 'more disgusting things than ever before encountered in Aldershot'.

Inspired by the pioneer example of the Daniells, the Wesleyans opened a Soldiers' Home in Aldershot which is listed on the 1871 census. This was followed by a similar establishment managed by the Church of England, and there were other signs of growing religious awareness, too. The ancient parish church of St Michael was enlarged in the 1860s, a Roman Catholic mission opened, and a synagogue was established for Jewish traders and soldiers.

The Daniells had concentrated their efforts on saving men from the effects of venereal disease, alcoholism and general immorality. They later extended this to saving the 'respectable' poor in the town, mainly the wives and children of the soldiers who lived 'off the strength' in the West End of the town. The 1871 census lists many of these families in the Queens Road and Albert Road areas. However, her attitude towards the prostitutes was hard and uncompromising, and she considered them beyond redemption. Some of these 'unfortunate' females may have been amongst the 50 all-female inmates of the Lock Hospital on the Farnham Road; their ages ranged from 16 to 45 years old.

28   The Presbyterian Church and Manse, photographed in about 1900. The Manse has long been demolished, but the church survives and was one of the earliest built in civilian Aldershot, bearing the date of 1863 in its stonework.

The establishment of several churches in the town also took place during this period. One of the earliest was the Presbyterian Church, whose construction was first proposed in 1861. A site was acquired in Victoria Road at a cost of £210, and building commenced in 1863, the date being recorded in the stonework of the building to this day, although the first service was not held in the building until six years later in 1869. Three years later it was felt there was the need for another church in the town to supplement the old St Michael's parish church, which was too small to cater for the growing population and was, in any case, situated in a somewhat isolated location, at some distance from the nucleus of the new town. In these circumstances the decision to build a church in the town centre was taken; the new building would be dedicated to the Holy Trinity. The land for the church between Arthur Street and Victoria Road was donated by Richard Allden, a leading resident of

Aldershot from the days before the arrival of the Army. After sufficient funds had been subscribed, the foundation stone was laid by the Bishop of Winchester in 1875, leading in due course to the consecration of the church in 1878.

At much the same time the Methodist Church on Grosvenor Road was also under construction. Begun in 1874, its first service was held two years later; situated on rising ground at the top of the long straight stretch of Victoria Road, the building to this day occupies a position of pre-eminence in the town, although it has now been converted into office use. Neither was the Roman Catholic Church slow in reacting to the needs of its flock. In 1872 a 'temporary' iron church was erected in Queen's Road, which actually saw service until 1912 when it was replaced by St Joseph's, which still serves the Roman Catholic community in Aldershot today.

29 Holy Trinity Church seen right in 1958. The foundation stone was laid in 1875 and the church was consecrated three years later.

30 The first Roman Catholic church in the town was the 'temporary' structure below, erected in 1872, which survived for 40 years until replaced by St Joseph's, which still stands today.

31 The Rotunda Church at the junction of Albert Road and Victoria Road in about 1910. Built in 1876 this was the home of the Primitive Methodists until the union of the Methodist churches when it was sold to the Reformed Episcopal Church of England. Adjoining can be seen the Primitive Methodist Soldiers' Home and Institute, built in 1887.

As the spiritual needs of the population were being addressed, so too were the educational needs of the children of the town. Until 1872 there only existed a number of private schools, although at different times there were upwards of a dozen of these in existence. Their facilities would have been very basic and uninspiring by the standards of today, but their importance should not be underestimated when the general lack of education up to this point meant that a large proportion of the population could neither read nor write. In January of 1872 the Aldershot School Board met for the

first time and later that year they took over the running both of Mrs. Paine's school in North Town and of the Church of England School at the bottom of Redan Road, which had originally been opened in 1854, the year of the Army's arrival in Aldershot. Other schools now began to appear in the town, reflecting the growth in educational provision across the country as a whole; in 1873 the School Board opened a school in West End, while the following year another one was opened to cater for the needs of the children in the East End of the town.

The commercial life of the town was also developing during this period. By 1861, when the Army had been in Aldershot for seven years, the town had developed in a somewhat haphazard manner, with several speculative builders undertaking developments in places they considered to be likely to offer the best return on their investments. As a result, more than one 'town centre' grew up—at Middle Hill, or at the junction of what is now High Street and Wellington Street, or in West End, or at what is now Ordnance Road. However, by the end of the 1870s a new generation of buildings was beginning to replace the earlier premises erected during the 1850s. These new buildings reflected the increased prosperity of the town, and some of them are still standing today, or are remembered with fondness by those inhabitants old enough to recall the town before the redevelopment of the 1960s and 1970s. One of the roads to change its character

quite substantially during this mid-Victorian phase of rebuilding was Victoria Road. From being a largely residential road, lined with houses boasting generous front gardens, it evolved over a period of years into something resembling the busy commercial road which exists today.

Perhaps one of the most enduring land-marks in Aldershot is the Cambridge Military Hospital, situated at the top of Gun Hill. The hospital was opened in 1879, and marked a major step forward in the field of military medical care. Before the 1870s only a series of small regimental hospitals existed, so the opening of the new hospital, complete with 260 beds, represented a radically new departure in the area of military hospital provision. The hospital cost £45,000 to build, which for the time was a not insignificant amount, and is named after the Duke of Cambridge, who performed the opening ceremony.

32 West End Junior School, now the home of the West End Centre. The school was one of many built around the turn of the century, following the passing of the Education Act of 1870.

Victoria Road in about 1890. The twin towers of the Presbyterian Church are clearly visible right of centre, but the street is still very much residential in character, and has yet to be developed commercially.

34 The same scene approximately twenty-five years later, and commercialisation has clearly begun. The Post Office has been built beyond the Aldershot Institute and shops have appeared in what had been the front gardens of houses on both sides of the road.

35 An artist's impression from 1882 of the Capital and Counties Bank in Victoria Road. The building still serves the same function as Lloyd's Bank, while the tower in the background belongs to the Aldershot Brewery.

But perhaps *the* outstanding feature in Aldershot and its environs is the statue of the Duke of Wellington. Over the years it has come to represent Aldershot, most notably in the logos of the Aldershot Civic Trust and the Wellington Press of Gale and Polden. However, the statue was not designed for an Aldershot location as the 'Iron Duke' died in 1852 before the Camp was established, and the eventual siting of the statue in Aldershot rescued the government of the day from an embarrassing situation. Matthew Cotes Wyatt, the sculptor of the Wellington Statue, was a member of the well-known architectural dynasty whose family included his father, James Wyatt, famous as a country house builder—his work included the infamous Fonthill Abbey (for William Beckford) where the tower spectacularly collapsed in 1825 owing to inadequate foundations. James was known latterly as 'Wyatt the Destroyer' from his sometimes unsympathetic restorations of old churches. It was decided during the Duke of Wellington's lifetime to erect a monument in order 'to commemorate the bravery of the British Hero, the skill of the British Artist and the gratitude of the British Nation'. Matthew Cotes Wyatt was appointed sculptor of the Duke of Wellington's statue thanks to the influence of the Duke of Rutland, who was chairman of the committee of subscribers commissioning the project. Rutland considered that Wyatt was one of the greatest English

36 Further evidence of the commercialisation of Victoria Road in the form of the *Victoria Hotel*. The hotel was one of the best in the town, but closed in 1966 and the site is now occupied by a row of shops.

37 The massive statue of the Duke of Wellington and his horse Copenhagen weighs 40 tons and stood at Hyde Park Corner in London from 1846 to 1885, when it was moved to Aldershot.

38   The Cambridge Military Hospital pictured not long after its construction in 1879. The hospital provided 260 beds and represented a radical departure in military hospital provision as hitherto no hospital of such a size had been in existence.

39   The workforce of Messrs. Martin, Wells and Co., pictured in the last years of the 19th century, possibly during the building of Gale and Polden's works in Birchett Road. Martin, Wells and Co. built many of Aldershot's landmarks which survive to this day, including the Cambridge Military Hospital; they also assisted with the re-erection of the Wellington Statue at Aldershot in 1885.

sculptors of all time, and had already employed him previously. The decision was not a popular one, but Queen Victoria gave her consent in 1839, and all went well until the disastrous decision was taken to place the statue on top of Decimus Burton's unfinished Triumphal Arch at Hyde Park Corner. Burton was not consulted and thought, rightly, that it would ruin the arch's appearance.

In 1846 the statue was erected on top of the arch and was immediately greeted by howls of derision; no work of art erected in London had ever received such ridicule. Questions were asked in Parliament and every newspaper denounced it; Wyatt himself wondered if it might look better at the new Wellington College in Berkshire. Later in the year the decision was taken to remove the statue, but the Duke of Wellington let it be known that he wanted the statue to remain and he would regard its removal as a deliberate snub to himself. There it remained

until 1883 when it was taken down as part of a proposed road improvement scheme and dumped in Green Park. It became an embarrassment to the Government who wished to remove it from London and give it to some provincial town. After more controversy another committee was formed, chaired by the Prince of Wales, to advise on the disposal of the statue. Eventually it was decided that Aldershot, home of the British Army, would be an ideal home for the bronze image of the Army's greatest commander. In 1884 work began on moving the statue and preparing it for transport. It was decided to dismember the statue as the horse weighed 33 tons and its rider seven tons. The journey to Aldershot took nearly four days by road using two carts, one drawn by four horses carrying the 'body' of Wellington, and another drawn by three horses containing the 'horse's' head, tail and body.

Aided by the Army, an Aldershot firm of building contractors, Messrs. Martin, Wells and Co. (who had also built the Cambridge Military Hospital some six years earlier), moved the pieces to Round Hill where the statue was reassembled. It was erected on a new red stone plinth bearing the name 'Wellington' on either side, and was surrounded by 16 old cannon barrels partially sunk into the surrounding hilltop. The statue overlooked the entrance to the Long Valley, site of many army manoeuvres, and was directly opposite Queen Victoria's Royal Pavilion. The site had been chosen by the Prince of Wales in conjunction with Queen Victoria's uncle, the Duke of Cambridge, who was commander of the British Army. On 19 August, with much military ceremony including representatives of every unit in Aldershot, the statue was formally handed over to Lieutenant-General D. Anderson, Commander of the Aldershot Division. Two companies of Infantry, two squadrons of Cavalry, a battery of Royal Horse Artillery and one company from the Medical Staff Corps and the Commissariat and Transport Corps comprised the military representation.

40 Aldershot's first horse-drawn fire engine, pictured in the last years of the 19th century. The driver is Mr. Austin, whose descendants still live in the town.

41 The Fire Station stood next to the Town Hall on Grosvenor Road and was built in 1904.

time the statue was being cast, Copenhagen had died (his heart is buried at the Duke's country house at Stratfield Saye between Reading and Basingstoke), and the horse used as a model was actually a mare called Rosemary!

Further evidence of the growing self-confidence (or perhaps self-preservation) of the town can be obtained from the establishment of the Fire Brigade in 1887. Initially manned by volunteers only, its equipment was at first rudimentary, but as time went by the standard of the equipment improved along with the technology available. The area served by the Brigade also expanded to include outlying areas such as the villages of Tongham, Ash and Seale. Yet there was still an agricultural presence in Aldershot among the new trades and businesses established since 1854. On the edge of the town, for example, lay West End Farm, and several agricultural labourers were listed in 1871 as living nearby. In Ayling House, Richard Stovold, aged 55, his wife and three servants lived off his profits as a landowner. Brickyards, such as the one in Cranmore Lane, still existed, too, doubtless to cater for the unceasing demand for building materials.

An enduring local legend exists which may well be apocryphal, but which maintains that during the reassembly, one of the workmen left his lunch inside the body of the statue, and upon returning from a break found his food inextricably sealed forever within the statue's innards. Less well known is that the horse on which Wellington sits is not strictly speaking the famous Copenhagen who carried him at the Battle of Waterloo in 1815; by the

As the century drew towards its close, followed shortly afterwards by the end of the Victorian era, Aldershot stood poised to move forward on the next stage of its development. The year 1894 would prove to be an important one in its history for a variety of reasons.

Chapter Four

Late Victorian and Edwardian Aldershot

The year 1894 marked a turning point in the development of the town and was in some respects arguably the most important since the arrival of the Army forty years earlier. The Aldershot of the 1890s was a prosperous place with a population of some 25,000 souls, a far cry from the tiny village of the 1850s. Two events were to occur within 12 months of each other which demonstrated that the town was ready to take its place alongside the hundreds of other, similar-sized towns the length and breadth of the country.

The first of these occurrences was made possible by the passing of the Local Government Act of 1894, which converted the Local Board into the Aldershot Urban District Council. With Urban District status, Aldershot now had a much greater control over its own destiny, and this stirred the first desires to try and attain the status of municipal borough, although this was not to be achieved until after the First World War. One example of the improvements the Urban District Council was able to bring to the town came in

42 All Saints' Garrison Church, Farnborough Road, pictured in about 1910. The church is popularly known as the 'Red Church' because of its redbrick construction, and was built in 1863.

43 St George's Garrison Church, Queen's Avenue, photographed in about 1900. The foundation stone was laid by Queen Victoria in 1892.

44 A view of Army Headquarters, Aldershot District, situated in Steeles Road, in the early years of the 20th century.

45 The Officers' Mess, Corunna Barracks in Stanhope Lines, photographed in about 1900.

46 & 47 Two photographs of Hospital Hill in the last years of the 19th century, the first looking away from civilian Aldershot, the second looking towards the civilian town. In the latter, the tower of the Grosvenor Road Methodist Church is clearly visible, while the barrack blocks in both photographs are those of Talavera Barracks.

48 A print taken from a photograph dating from the late 19th century. The church spire on the right belongs to St George's Garrison Church on Queen's Avenue.

the matter of street lighting. Hitherto, this had been of the gas or oil-fuelled variety which had been less than effective in dispelling what must have been a near Stygian gloom, at least in certain areas of the town. After a trial of a single electric lamp erected by the Incandescent Light Company in Station Road in 1894, it was decided to extend the provision of such lighting to the other main roads in the town.

Other benefits were to follow in later years, as the powers invested in the Council were increased. The passing of the Education Act of 1902 devolved the responsibility for elementary education onto the Urban District Councils, and in the case of Aldershot this resulted in the formation of the Education Committee in 1903. The years following this development saw the opening of the Newport Road School in 1905 and of the Aldershot County Secondary School in 1912, although

the opening of schools within the town was not exactly a new phenomenon, West End Infants' School having been opened in 1898.

The other major event of the year actually had its origins a generation earlier, and some sixty miles away in Kent. In 1893 the firm of Gale and Polden began an association with Aldershot that was to last for nearly ninety years and provide the town with its own newspaper which is still successfully serving the local community over a hundred years later. The firm itself was begun in about 1868 in Chatham by James Gale as a stationer's shop with a small printing works attached; when Mr. Gale was joined in partnership by the two brothers Ernest and Russell Polden, the firm that was to find world-wide fame as printers and publishers was well and truly established. In 1893 a branch was opened in Wellington Street, and later the same year the decision was taken to build a factory in Aldershot. Land was sought and duly

49 The General Post Office, situated at the junction of Victoria Road and Station Road. It was built in 1902, and is a good example of Edwardian exuberance in architectural design.

50 The Town Hall in Grosvenor Road was built in 1904 and designed by C.E. Hutchinson. It is a building typical of its date and was to be the scene of many civic ceremonies during the next 70 years.

51 Grosvenor Road, formerly named Bank Street, looking towards the Methodist Church. Taken at the turn of the century, this shows a mainly residential street. Note the two forms of transport—horse-drawn and motorised.

52 Grosvenor Road looking north towards its junction with High Street. The cavalry barracks gates are just visible in the background, and the bustling street scene is in marked contrast to the previous picture taken approximately thirty years before.

53   Gale and Polden's Wellington Works on the corner of Birchett Road and The Grove were devastated by a serious fire in July 1918, yet production of *The Aldershot News* was scarcely affected by the disaster.

54   Firemen struggling to contain the blaze at the Wellington Works in 1918.

found on which to erect the factory; the site was occupied by a market garden on the corner of Birchett Road and The Grove, and the same builders who had built the Cambridge Military Hospital and helped erect the Wellington Statue, Messrs. Martin, Wells and Co., were engaged to build the factory. The printing presses were transported by rail from Chatham, having been kept running until the last possible moment, and upon arrival at their new Aldershot home, they were loaded into the factory through large windows looking onto The Grove. Before the first floor had even been completed, the machines on the ground floor were set busily to work.

Now that the necessary machinery was in place, the plan to publish a new weekly newspaper, *The Aldershot News*, was put into operation. The first issue saw the light of day on 23 June 1894, but had been a month in the planning. The intention was to produce a newspaper providing all the local news for the town and surrounding areas, as well as producing a military gazette for the Army, wherever it was stationed throughout the British Empire. The success of these aims can perhaps best be gauged by the fact that the first issue sold its entire print run of 12,000 copies within 24 hours with a further 4,000 copies being retained for despatch to the four corners of the globe. The 12,000 copies sold in Aldershot represented a copy for one man, woman and child out of every two which, even allowing for the curiosity value attached to a new enterprise, was still no small achievement. The influence of a local newspaper on the community it serves cannot be underestimated and, although *Sheldrake's Aldershot and Sandhurst Military Gazette* (to give it its full title) had been appearing weekly since 1859, the *Aldershot News* very quickly demonstrated that it was here to stay, and eventually saw off its older rival. Gale and Polden continued in Aldershot, surviving a disastrous fire in the process, but they could not outlive the attentions of the Robert Maxwell empire. Taken over by him, the firm

55 Early Foden steam trucks pictured at the Aldershot and District Traction Company Works in Grosvenor Road in the early 1900s. An open-topped double-decker bus is just visible to the right of the trucks.

was closed down as part of a streamlining exercise in 1981.

If Gale and Polden were to have a lasting influence on the town, so too would the Aldershot and District Traction Company, which was founded in 1912. The first two double-decker motorised buses had appeared some six years previously and were operated by the Aldershot and Farnborough Motor Omnibus Company. They had been purchased in St Leonards-on-Sea and driven from there to Aldershot, the 80-mile journey taking nine hours to complete. The service provided by the two vehicles in effect comprised a journey from Farnham to Farnborough via Aldershot, each bus doing one 'leg' of the journey. The new, motorised buses soon saw off their horse-drawn competitors and the company gradually began to expand its operations, opening a new route to Farnham and one to Ash and Deepcut. If the company was to expand any further, however, capital was now required. The solution arrived in 1912 when the British Automobile Traction Company Ltd. joined with the Aldershot company to form the Aldershot and District Traction Company Ltd. The new concern, or

'Traco' as it became affectionately known, would eventually build up a network of routes which at its peak would cover much of central Southern England. In the two years of peace remaining before the outbreak of the First World War services were quickly expanded and towns now served by the company included Fleet, Camberley, Haslemere, Guildford, Dorking and Leatherhead.

As the town grew in size, so did its recreational facilities. As has already been mentioned, theatres and music halls appeared on the scene at a very early point, but these were of a very rough and ready nature, many of them simply the 'back room' attached to drinking houses. As time progressed more permanent establishments were built, and in tandem with this permanence there was a corresponding increase in the professionalism of the performances, too. A map dated 1875 shows the Alexandra Music Hall situated near Miss Daniell's Soldiers' Home, and the Apollo Music Hall at the top of Union Street burned down in 1889, leading to the Theatre Royal being built two years later at the junction of Birchett Road and Gordon Road.

56 The Theatre Royal which stood on the corner of Birchett Road and Gordon Road, pictured in 1945. Its site is now a car sales room and garage.

57 Station Road looking towards the Hippodrome Theatre in Edwardian times. The *South Western Hotel* is on the right.

But perhaps the event for which Aldershot is best remembered in this area of activity is the stage debut of Charlie Chaplin at the tender age of five years old in 1894. His parents were both music hall artistes, and his mother on this particular occasion was on stage at the Canteen, a theatre whose location has now sadly been lost but which Chaplin himself described as 'grubby' and 'mean'. During her performance, Mrs. Chaplin's voice cracked and then died away to little more than a whisper. Unsurprisingly, given the rowdy nature of the audience, boos and catcalls ensued; in order to plug the gap caused by Mrs. Chaplin's incapacity the young Charlie, waiting in the wings for his mother to finish her act, was pushed onto the stage, the stage manager having previously heard him perform for friends. He began singing a well-known

song of the day called 'Jack Jones' and before he had finished a shower of coins began landing on the stage. Charlie obviously knew when he was on to a good thing, and started collecting up the money, telling the audience he would do this first and sing afterwards, which caused great amusement amongst the patrons.

The stage manager then appeared and began collecting the money, much to Charlie's consternation, as he evidently thought he was about to be deprived of his just rewards; he even followed the manager off the stage and was only satisfied when he saw the money was safely handed over to his mother. Upon his return to the stage he says he felt 'quite at home' and sang a few songs, danced and did several imitations. One of these was of his mother, and the lad's voice cracked in much

58 A view down Station Road during the First World War with the Hippodrome Theatre on the left. Two tea rooms, the cupola of the Post Office and the Palace Cinema can be seen, while in the distance the outline of the Cambridge Military Hospital can just be made out.

59 Municipal munificence. The gardens in Grosvenor Road taken in the 1930s with the Town Hall in the background. The tower of the Methodist Church is also visible.

the same way as his mother's had earlier in the evening, which of course provoked much laughter. Eventually, his mother returned to carry him off the stage, this time to a storm of applause (and more coin throwing). In his autobiography, Chaplin reflected, 'that night was my first appearance on the stage and mother's last'.

As the 19th century gave way to the 20th, improvements in the town's facilities and utilities gathered pace. The Isolation Hospital was opened in 1900, and three years later the Council assumed responsibility for the town's electricity supply. Four years after that, in 1907, a major improvement was started with the surfacing of the main roads in the town with tarmac. Until then, they were muddy in wet weather, and dusty in dry, and many of the more heavily used roads had 'sunk' to a level two or three feet below their verges. In 1904 the Town Hall in Grosvenor Road was opened, together with the Fire Station next door, and now Aldershot had municipal buildings befitting the status acquired a decade earlier. The Urban District Council had also bought the land adjoining their new offices from the Parish in 1895, and now they set about turning the land into a more pleasant area for rest and relaxation. Accordingly, in 1905, a tree planting ceremony known as 'Arbour Day' was held when the prominent citizens who had donated them planted 32 trees.

Indeed, by the 1890s gentrification had begun and several areas of Aldershot contained properties built to house the growing numbers of the upper middle classes who were making their home in the town. One such area was Cargate, which derives its name from 'Cartgate', the old western approach to Aldershot village. The 1568 Crondall Customary contains references to 'Cargate feald' and a 'close called the Carte Gate'. On the first military Ordnance Survey map of 1856 Cargate Copse is one of several wooded areas marked. In the 1870s and 1880s this high ground was covered with a residential area of fine houses in well laid out

grounds with ample plantations, and the roads were named Cargate Hill, Cargate Grove, Cargate Terrace and Cargate Avenue. In this last named road in 1891 lived some of the more prosperous families of Aldershot. The houses had names such as 'Mossgill', which was home to local builder George Kemp, his wife, daughter and servant. Adjacent to this household was an architect named Samuel Friend, also with wife, daughter, servant and a lodger. 'The Laurels' housed Frederick Tuplin, a solicitor with wife, family and servants. Two nearby properties housed George Digby, a licensed dealer and manager of a furniture store with the full complement of family and supporting servants, and Henry Sheppard who held a similar position supplying furnishings to the military camp. Also in Cargate Avenue lived Henry Wyatt, vicar of the nearby Surrey parish of Wyke, and an Army Captain, his wife, two sons and as many as four servants (most of the Cargate households contained only one or two servants). At 'The Elms' dwelt a widow, Mary Moseley, 'living on her own means' with her four daughters. Although all the households contained servants who 'lived in', they were probably also served by others who came in on a daily basis.

Part of the attraction of the Cargate site for housing is its elevated position, and therefore it is not surprising that at the top of Cargate Hill is the reservoir of the former Mid Southern Utility Company and the water tower, built in 1907, which today is still one of the dominant landmarks of the Aldershot landscape. Areas such as the tree-lined residential Church Lane West and Eggars Hill also contain some of Aldershot's most prestigious residences, built to take advantage of the fine views across the Surrey hills as far as Hindhead. These houses also stand in their own grounds, and have carriage drives and facilities for stabling.

In stark contrast to all this opulence on the edge of the town, the centre of Aldershot contained streets of artisans' dwellings. An example of these was to be found in the parallel streets

60 The Cottage Hospital, *c.*1900. The hospital stood at the junction of Church Lane East and St George's Road. The foundation stone was laid in 1896, but after the opening of Frimley Park Hospital in the 1970s the buildings were demolished. The Church of Latter Day Saints now stands on the site.

61 Upper-middle-class housing in Cargate Avenue in the early 1900s, a good example of the gentrification of the town.

62 Another view of Cargate Avenue in the early 1900s.

of Crimea Road and Sebastopol Road where many of the properties housed more than one family. Typical male occupants were mainly labourers, and the 1891 census lists a cabman, a gunsmith, a blacksmith, a coachman, a groom and a shirt collar maker. A few of the females followed occupations such as dressmaker, laundress or milliner, but the majority of the wives (including some soldiers' wives who lodged there) were engaged in raising their children and did not work outside the home.

From the very first days of the Army arriving in Aldershot, Royalty had played an important part in its development. Prince Albert in particular had been deeply involved in many of the early initiatives, not least of

which was the siting and subsequent construction of the Royal Pavilion. Queen Victoria herself was a frequent visitor to the Camp, and as the 19th century drew to a close, members of foreign royal families also paid several visits to Aldershot. Two of the earliest such visitors were King Leopold of the Belgians and Prince Oscar of Sweden who stayed with Queen Victoria and Prince Albert at the Royal Pavilion in 1856. As time went by, the visiting dignitaries would include Tsar Alexander II of Russia in 1874, and 15 years later would come Kaiser Wilhelm II of Germany in 1889—the same 'Kaiser Bill' for whose blood the popular press would clamour in 1918. Other later and perhaps more exotic

63 The Royal Review of 1913. HM King George V accompanied by General Sir Douglas Haig ride across Queen's Parade with Queen's Avenue in the background.

64 Cavalry training in the Long Valley between 1904 and 1906. The date of the photograph was established from the style of the uniforms—the NCOs and men are wearing the khaki service dress and peaked caps introduced in 1902 and 1904 respectively.

65 Sunday Church parades were a regular feature of Army life. Here, the 3rd Hussars are parading down Wellington Avenue, preceded by the band.

visitors included the Shah of Persia in 1919, and two years later saw the arrival of Crown Prince Hirohito of Japan, who as Emperor would preside over Japan's sorry role in the Second World War.

But perhaps the most significant event involving Royalty, at least insofar as the nation as a whole was concerned, centred upon our own King Edward VII in 1902. On 14 June the King and Queen Alexandra attended a Searchlight Tattoo in the grounds of Government House, during which the King was unfortunate enough to contract a chill which necessitated him being taken back to London the following day. The Coronation Review of all the troops stationed in Aldershot was scheduled to take place on 16 June, and the event was forced to go ahead in the absence of the King with the salute being taken by the Queen. Instead of getting better, the King's condition took a turn for the worse and eight days after the Review it was decided to postpone the Coronation until 9 August, when eventually it all went according to plan.

If Aldershot was the home of formal reviews and parades, presided over by all manner of royalty, it was also the scene of many other parades of less importance which had become almost routine in nature. Sunday church parades were held by all units and they must have presented a colourful sight indeed in the full splendour of their dress uniforms. The marching men would be accompanied by military bands, and the whole event would be eagerly watched by hundreds of locals, and indeed not-so-locals. Sundays were not the only occasion when large crowds would turn out to witness a parade of troops. Units returning from service overseas, perhaps having seen action, would also march from the railway station to their new barracks, again usually accompanied by appropriate music from the band. The returning troops would sometimes bear some memento or trophy, gained in the course of their duties in the Empire. In 1903, the 14th King's Hussars attracted a great deal of interest upon their return from the Boer War in South Africa, as their new mascot, a baboon named 'Kruger', seemed quite happy to walk along beside the troops on their march from the station to the West Cavalry Barracks. History does not record if Kruger was able to keep in step with his human brothers in arms!

66 Another church parade outside St George's Church, Queen's Avenue in about 1910. The two small boys in the foreground are Edmund and Alfred Moss, father and uncle of local resident Mrs. Sally Lawrence, née Moss.

67 A view of Queen's Avenue, looking south in about 1900. The spire of St George's Garrison Church is visible in the distance.

68 An illustration from *The Builder* magazine of 1907 showing the proposed extension of St Michael's Church, designed by Sir T.G. Jackson.

69 St Michael's Church taken from Manor Park with the new nave and north aisle of 1910-11. The south-west tower, built of Bagshot conglomerate and brick, was erected in the 17th century.

70 A view of the chancel and choir of St Michael's Church taken from the west gallery in about 1911.

71 A similar view from a few years later, showing the rood screen.

72 The Palace Cinema in Station Road. The photograph was taken in 1913, hence the original caption to the photograph of 'New Picture Palace'.

73 In Wellington Street stood John Farmer's first shoe shop, pictured with the owner and staff lined up outside. Adjacent are the premises of Park and Sparkhall whose arcade linked Wellington Street to High Street.

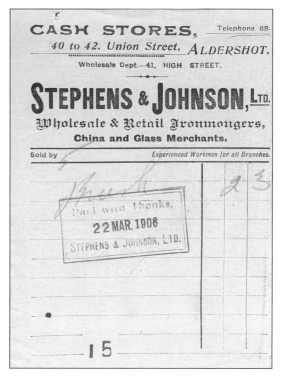

74 A receipt of 1906 for a 2s. 3d. brush from Stephens and Johnson, complete with a two figure telephone number.

75 In High Street were the premises of Stephens and Johnson, ironmongers, also pictured with staff and goods lined up outside. The premises are now empty although there are plans to turn the site into a visitor centre for Aldershot.

76 Delivery vehicles were a feature of life in small towns. Here is John Pooley in the pony and trap of H. Uglow, greengrocers, taken in Queen's Road.

77 No. 1, Station Road, the shop of McDowell, saddler and harness supplier, pictured in 1894. Mr. John McDowell and Mr. Sharpe are pictured in the doorway. The Aldershot Public Library now stands on the site. Emily McDowell, daughter of John, taught at Newport Road School from its opening.

78 & 79 Two views of Union Street looking towards Wellington Street in the early years of the 20th century. The first is taken from the top of Union Street while the second is taken from about half-way down. The first one certainly gives the impression of a thriving, bustling thoroughfare, and it is hard to believe that, less than 50 years earlier, this site would have been nothing more than windswept heath-land.

80 Union Street in the years after the First World War. The shop signs bear testimony to the wide range of goods available and, although motor cars predominate, the horse-drawn vehicles had not been completely forced off the roads.

81   Wellington Street looking towards High Street in the 1890s. The traffic is all horse-drawn, and the pace of life appears to be altogether slower than it is today!

82   Open spaces—Redan Hill with Edwardian picnickers in the foreground. Military Aldershot is just visible in the right background.

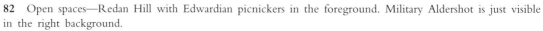

83 Recreational activities—in 1910, the 2nd Aldershot Scout Troop gathered in Aldershot Station yard to parade before attending the Scout Rally in Windsor Great Park. Mr. Toye is the scoutmaster.

84 The 2nd Aldershot Scouts in 1913 pictured at the Scout Hut, Salamanca Barracks, Hospital Hill.

85   St Joseph's School, Queen's Road. The class is Standard II photographed in 1905.

86   Farnborough Road pictured in 1914. The location is approximately fifty yards north of the junction with Wellington Avenue, and the Scottish Rifles have the Cavalry Barracks gates on their left.

Chapter Five

The First World War and After

The bullets fired by Gavrilo Princip into the Archduke Franz Ferdinand of Austria in the Serbian town of Sarajevo on 28 June 1914 must have seemed a very remote and inconsequential affair at the time, yet the repercussions of this act of assassination would affect the whole world in the shape of the First World War. As the foremost Army base in the country, Aldershot was bound to witness a proportionally greater drama played out in its environs than almost anywhere else in the country.

For seven weeks of almost constant sunshine, Europe stumbled towards war, apparently without anyone able to do much to avoid it. When war was finally declared on 4 August, thousands of territorials poured into the town, many of whom had simply reported for duty without having even waited for the arrival of their official call-up papers. With such vast numbers of extra troops in the town, the Army found itself scarcely able to cope, and as a result a series of tented encampments sprang up in the surrounding countryside to cater for the extra men. Great secrecy surrounded the movements of troops in the early days of the war. *The Aldershot News* carried no mention of which units were in the town, or had already left it; instead, the newspaper contained a plethora of reports detailing the theft of bicycles! Perhaps such occurrences were endemic and in normal times would have been considered too prosaic to warrant much attention; now they were gratefully seized upon as a means of

filling valuable column inches! As the first troops left the town, mobilisation was still far from complete, with large numbers of men pouring in to replace those who had left. Such was the secrecy surrounding the departing forces that even the train drivers were not told their destination until immediately before the signal to leave was given.

By the end of the first month of the war, the reality of the situation had begun to hit home. On 30 August, the first train arrived from Southampton carrying some two hundred wounded soldiers, injured during the first exchanges of hostilities at Mons, or on the retreat from there back towards le Cateau and beyond. The earliest first-hand accounts of the fighting were gleaned from these men, and it was in this way that the inhabitants of Aldershot received some of the first tidings from the front line.

Earlier in the month, on 8 August, the first great appeal for volunteers was made with Lord Kitchener asking for 100,000 volunteers in the 'grave National Emergency'. Such was the success of this appeal that recruiting offices all over the country were quite simply swamped by the numbers of men—and boys—clamouring to get at the 'Boche' before the adventure was over by Christmas, as everybody seemed to agree it would be. Aldershot became one of the principal centres for the reception and training of these recruits and, if the recruiting offices were overwhelmed by the numbers involved, then so too was the

Army itself. Equipment of all kinds was not available in the necessary quantities; troops would drill in civilian clothes, or perhaps in a mixture of uniforms; weaponry training could often only be carried out using obsolete rifles; and kit bags would arrive at infrequent intervals and long after the arrival of the men themselves. Nevertheless, within a few months these civilians were trained into an army deemed sufficiently capable to be dispatched to the great mincing machine that was the Western Front or, as the conflict wore on, to Gallipoli or Mesopotamia or whichever theatre of operations required their services. In order to accommodate the influx of new arrivals, the East and West End Schools were requisitioned to accommodate the men of Kitchener's Army, those volunteers who had flocked to the colours in such vast numbers in the first, over-confident days of the war. Many of them would find the battlefields of the Somme, or Ypres, or Gallipoli their final resting places.

A kind of routine settled on Aldershot as the war progressed. A consignment of mixed factory workers, farm labourers or perhaps office workers with the odd stockbroker thrown in for good measure would arrive at the railway station, they would spend a few months being trained to meet the rigours of trench warfare,

after which they would be sent to the Front, only to be replaced by a fresh delivery of hopeful young men. Many returned home, however, badly scarred and disfigured by the wounds they had sustained fighting the enemy. Some even began to question whether the skill of surgeons in saving their lives was justified if it meant they had to eke out their lives away from the public gaze, so horrible were their injuries. An attempt to address this problem was begun at the Cambridge Military Hospital towards the end of 1915 when a small unit under the auspices of Sir William Arbuthnot Lane was established for the purposes of repairing facial and head injuries. The leading light in this new venture was a young New Zealander, Harold Delf Gillies, and he and his colleagues were to achieve remarkable results in repairing the damaged faces of their patients, devising new techniques for this purpose and improving existing methods as they did so. In short, the birth of plastic surgery in this country took place under Gillies and the rest of the team in the Cambridge Military Hospital. The unit soon outgrew its premises in the hospital, however, and in 1918 it was transferred to Queen Mary's Hospital at Sidcup in Kent, but by then the knowledge gained by the team was being extended to include burns, injuries

87 A detachment of the Women's Auxiliary Army Corps marching past King George V and Queen Mary as they take the salute on Queen's Parade in 1918. The WAAF were stationed in barracks at nearby Bordon.

88 The War Memorial in the Municipal Gardens is here flanked by two captured First World War guns, one Turkish, the other German. They were removed in 1940.

to limbs and congenital malformations. At the outbreak of the Second World War, the now Sir Harold Delf Gillies and his team were to achieve even more success; one of these team members was Gillies' cousin, the legendary Sir Archibald McIndoe.

After more than four years of hostilities the guns finally fell silent at the eleventh hour of the eleventh day of the eleventh month of 1918. In Aldershot the moment was greeted cautiously at first, with people scarcely daring to believe that at last the nightmare was really over. A few flags and bunting appeared first, having been carefully prepared for just this occasion; a few people ventured onto the streets, until by midday they had become a huge

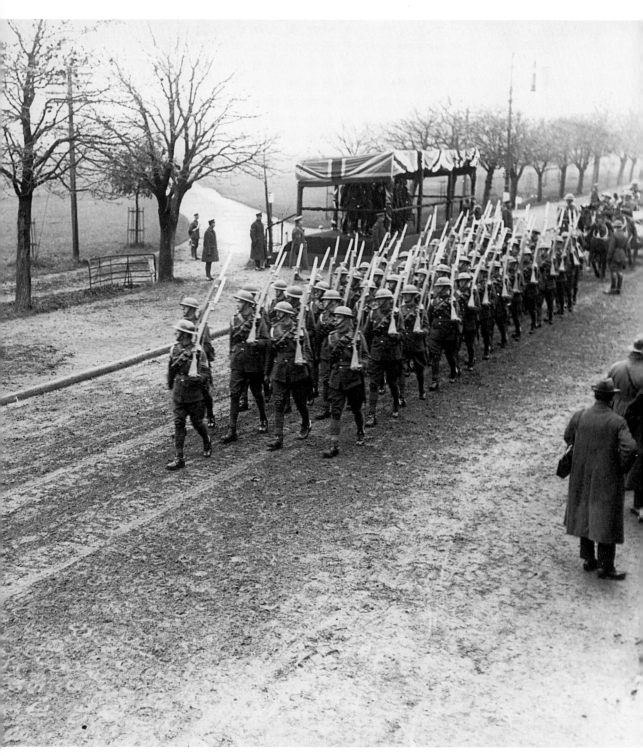

89 One of the many foreign visitors to Aldershot was the Shah of Persia. The Royal Engineers are here passing the saluting base on Queen's Avenue on 3 November 1919.

90   The Aldershot Incorporation Committee pictured in 1922 at the time Aldershot acquired Municipal Borough status.

crowd, civilians and servicemen alike. By then nearly all the shops had closed, the church bells were ringing, factory sirens were being sounded at irregular intervals and any vehicle attempting to negotiate the streets was instantly boarded by joyful revellers hitching a few yards' ride on the running board.

For Aldershot, as for every town and village throughout the country, the Armistice came as a huge relief, albeit tinged with sorrow, as hardly a family in the land had remained untouched by the war in one way or another. Yet in some respects, life continued much as it ever had in Aldershot. Troops still came and went, there was always some spot where the presence of the British Army was required, and returning men passed through the town prior to demobilisation; superficially, at least, little had changed.

In the years immediately following the cessation of hostilities one event stands out as a moment of great importance in the history and development of Aldershot. Although the early attempts to become a Municipal Borough came to nothing, the idea resurfaced during the latter stages of the First World War. A Development Committee had been formed in 1917 with a view to obtaining the Municipal Charter, but after making preliminary enquiries as to the feasibility of the scheme, its activities

ceased until the war came to an end. Matters began to move more rapidly in 1920, however, and an exploratory meeting was held in January of that year, which voted overwhelmingly in favour of the plan. A petition was organised and the views of householders in the town were sought; of these, 2,366 or nearly two-thirds supported the idea, while an opposing petition against the moves attracted only 22 signatures. Both petitions were presented to the Privy Council, and following a Public Inquiry under the chairmanship of Mr. T.R. Colquhoun Dill, the Charter for the Incorporation of Aldershot as a Municipal Borough was signed by King George V on 23 March 1922. It defined the boundaries of the new borough, and also specified the boundaries of the three wards which comprised the borough. Each of the three wards would return six councillors, and dates were fixed for the first elections to the new Council.

Charter Day was fixed for Wednesday, 21 June 1922. The occasion was a mixture of celebration on the one hand, and pomp and ceremony on the other. The day began with the Mayor-elect, Arthur Smith, and the Deputy Mayor-elect, Henry Ainger, travelling up to London by train to collect the Charter. At Waterloo station they were met by

91 Charter Day in 1922. Mr. R.J. Snuggs, Chairman of Aldershot Urban District Council, addresses Mayor-elect Mr. Arthur H. Smith. General the Rt. Hon. J.B. Seely, the Lord Lieutenant of Hampshire, is on the extreme right and Lt.-General Sir T.L.N. Morland, G.O.C. Aldershot Command is standing behind Mr. Smith.

an escort of 12 men under the command of RSM Lister of the Queen's Westminster Rifles, and on the return journey they were accompanied by the Rt. Hon. J.B. Seely, the Lord Lieutenant of Hampshire, and Lord Wolmer, Aldershot's M.P. At Aldershot railway station the Royal British Legion provided a guard of honour and the town itself was decked out with flags and bunting in honour of the occasion. The ceremony of presentation was to be held in Manor Park, with a procession through the streets of Aldershot from Talavera and Salamanca Barracks to the Park. The procession was made up of representatives from every military unit based in Aldershot, as well as every conceivable kind of civilian organisation, including those bearing civic, charitable, educational, service and business credentials. In the Park itself, great emphasis was placed on the future of Aldershot; after all, the ceremony did mark

the first page in a new chapter of the town's development. The children of the town were accorded pride of place in the proceedings, and they responded by cheering enthusiastically as each section of the procession passed into the Park. The whole procession took fully 20 minutes to enter, and as each speaker rose to address the crowd, the children again began to cheer enthusiastically. The remarks of the Mayor-elect, Arthur Smith were particularly aimed at the youngsters: 'Today concerns you even more than it concerns the older people of our town. You will understand, as you grow up, that it is very difficult to inspire the older people, but we have very good ground with the children.'

More of the same followed, exhorting the children to take pride in their town and generally to turn themselves into responsible citizens. He finished by harking back to Aldershot's early history:

The Manor House there, the old church behind it, and the grounds surrounding this place is the actual old history of Aldershot, and it is very fitting that this ceremony should take place on the most historic ground in Aldershot, and ground that is the property of the town for ever.

The day's celebrations were completed by a military display in the Park, and in the evening a banquet attended by over 200 guests was held in the Redan Drill Hall. These guests included a cross-section of the townspeople, as well as the Mayors of Guildford, Portsmouth, Southampton and Winchester, the Lord Lieu-

tenant of Hampshire, the Rt. Hon. J. Seely and the General Officer Commanding-in-Chief Aldershot Command, Lt.-General Sir Thomas Morland.

As a result of Aldershot's newly acquired status, the town was granted a Coat of Arms the following year. The arms of the Urban District Council had not been officially sanctioned, and consisted of a kind of visual pun, displaying an alder tree below three piles of cannon-balls, or shot. The new arms were a much more impressive design and were based on the arms of the Tichborne family who had owned the Manor of Aldershot from 1599 until

92 King George V and Queen Mary take the salute from the Highland Light Infantry in May 1928. The location is Farnborough Road outside the gates of the Royal Pavilion.

about 1750. Included in the new design were crossed swords to represent the Army and a mitre representing the Bishops of Winchester who had owned the Hundred of Crondall of which Aldershot had formed a part. Finally, the motto chosen was also that of the Tichborne family, 'Pugna pro Patria', which could hardly have been more appropriate since its translation from the Latin is 'Fight for your Country'.

One of the issues which the new Council needed to address was that of providing sufficient housing to fulfil David Lloyd George's pledge 'to make Britain a fit country for heroes to live in'. Before the First World War the census for Aldershot had shown a population of 35,175 in 1911. This figure was composed of a military population of 15,711 and a civilian one of 19,464. Ten years later the military population had fallen to a peacetime total of 9,501 whilst the civilian sector stayed steady at 19,253, making the total number of Aldershot residents 28,754. By 1931 the total population of Aldershot had risen to 34,280 and it is reasonable to suppose that the military section of the population would not have increased much given the continuing peaceful situation. This increase in the civilian population meant that new homes were needed and this resulted in a large building programme of houses in the area, and pressure for new modern housing. Nationally, 150,000 houses were being built on average each year during the 1920s of which a quarter were built by local authorities. During the 1930s this number increased, reaching its peak just short of 350,000 in 1936. Many of the new houses were in a different style, namely the three-bedroomed semi-detached. Unlike the Victorian and Edwardian terraces, this was low-density housing built on plots large enough to accommodate a front and a back garden. Typically they would be of two storeys with two living rooms and a kitchen downstairs, and three bedrooms and a bathroom upstairs. The kitchens and bathrooms would be fitted with the most modern equipment. Much of the building would have been in the hands of the private sector and done by small local speculative builders.

In Aldershot, many new roads such as Jubilee Road, Coronation Road and Elston Road were laid out in this new uniform style. An advertisement in *The Aldershot News* in January 1936 for the Manor Park Estate listed new houses for sale in Jubilee Road for £550, which required a total deposit of £35, although it was possible to secure one of these properties for as little as £5. These were being built by local builder F.H. Dyer, a local firm trading from a house on the corner of Boxalls Lane and Jubilee Road. Mr. Dyer then developed Coronation Road, where, in *The Aldershot News* of May 1937, similar new semi-detached houses were being advertised for £695, again with an initial deposit of £35 and a weekly repayment of 18s. 1d. For the privilege of owning a detached house in Evelyn Avenue the price had risen to £1,025, but for this sum one bought a house described as 'an ideal Gentleman's Residence', containing central heating, luxury bathroom, two WCs, two side entrances and a garage to take a full size car. In nearby Elston Road (named after John Elston, the first chairman in 1860 of the Aldershot Burial Board, who is buried in the municipal cemetery in Redan Road) houses cost a mere £495 according to an advertisement again in *The Aldershot News* of May 1936 placed by Kingham and Kingham, the local estate agents.

Many other former green fields and orchards in the area were developed into estates, such as the land owned by the Gillian family, which became Orchard Way, Gillian Avenue and Brighton Road. Here, some of the fruit trees from the original orchards were preserved in the gardens of the houses. Again, the builder built himself a house on the site, this time on the corner of Lower Farnham Road and Orchard Way. Houses on the western side of Lower Farnham Road, known as the Sunnyside Estate, were advertised for sale in this period for £600 by the builders J.M. Cuttill of Guildford. Some houses were built for rent, rather than for sale to individual buyers. In 1936 Lees the Builders advertised properties at 'moderate' rentals on the Crown estate which included Northbrook, Brockenhurst and Southmead Roads. For those who had purchased one of these new houses, and then found they needed to move on, there were arrangements such as the offer in the local paper in 1936 of 'a new semi-detached six room house in a select neighbourhood (Coronation Road) for 26 shillings per week inclusive, or the owner would consider transferring the mortgage for £25 down, as he was leaving the district.' In 1920 the Council purchased the Aldershot Park Estate and developed the area to the east of Lower Farnham Road as a council housing estate. The estate stretched to the Hampshire-Surrey county boundary and the River Blackwater. Roads on the estate were given names which had associations with local landowning families such as the Whytes and the Tichbornes. At the lower end of the estate, Gloucester Road was named for the Duke of Gloucester, who had many associations with the borough, and Morland Road was named after Lt.-Gen. Sir T.C.L. Morland, who was

93 The Aldershot Bathing Pool pictured in the 1930s. A good idea of the size of the pool can be gained from this picture.

94 Aldershot Swimming Club pictured in about 1935. The bathing pool was the envy of most towns throughout the south of England.

G.O.C. of Aldershot at the time of the grant of the Charter for the Incorporation of Aldershot as a Municipal Borough in 1922.

However, not all of the estate was covered in housing. The former avenue leading to the mansion was retained as The Avenue with new tree planting, and the houses were set well back from the road, leaving a wide grass verge. Two schools, Park Infants and Park Junior, were built to educate the children from the estate and the surrounding areas. The mansion house was retained and used for a variety of purposes. The former pleasure grounds, which contained a lake (which in the 1880s during the ownership of Mr. Charles D'Oridant was described as 'a fine sheet of water'), were converted into a public park. The lake became Aldershot Bathing Pool, frequently described as 'the finest in the South of England', and its

conversion and improvement was one of Aldershot Council's major improvement projects of the 1920s. The old lake was drained and its original shape retained. The necessary filtering plant, changing rooms and other amenities were built and the whole surrounding area was landscaped to form pleasant lawns and terraces. The project cost nearly £20,000, a considerable sum at the time. The Aldershot Swimming Club was formed to enjoy this amenity.

Even before the Second World War, space for new housing was becoming scarce in Aldershot. The town was hemmed in on two sides by the county boundary with Surrey, and on the other two sides by the land owned by the War Department. The local newspaper carried advertisements for the 'Aldershot Bungalow Estate' in 1937, which on closer inspection was being built across the county boundary in Oxenden Road, Tongham, 'near Ash'. There was also discussion in the same edition of the proposals for Aldershot to expand its territories across into Surrey, to give more space for development. In addition to the new bathing pool facilities in Aldershot Park, the 1920s and 1930s generally saw a growth in the leisure and sporting facilities available within the town. Of these, perhaps the foundation of Aldershot Football Club would create the greatest impact for, within five years of first kicking a ball, they found themselves in the Third Division (South) of the Football League, and in years to come they could truly describe themselves as players on the national stage.

In December 1926 a meeting was held in the Council Chamber at which various civic dignitaries including the Mayor were present, and it was agreed that a company should be formed in an attempt to start a football club.

Later in the same month an application to join the Southern League the following season was successfully made, and preparations could begin in earnest for the big kick-off in August. Permission from the Council to use the Recreation Ground was duly obtained by February, Angus Seed was appointed manager, and in due course a total of 14 professional players were signed, ready for the new club's first competitive match at home to Grays Thurrock on 27 August. A crowd of 3,500 were rewarded by a 4-0 victory and, although their opponents would eventually finish bottom of the league and were therefore arguably the weakest team in the table, this was of little consequence in the wake of this encouraging start. The team and supporters were soon brought back to earth with a bump when they lost the next game, also played at the Recreation Ground by 5-2 against Southampton Reserves. At the end of the season Aldershot stood in a

95 The captains of Aldershot and Grays Thurrock at the toss with the referee before the club's first game in 1927.

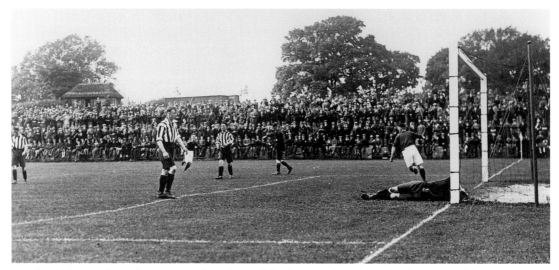

96 An Aldershot forward turns away from the goal having scored in the club's first competitive game against Grays Thurrock in 1927. Aldershot won the match 4-0.

97 An aerial view of the Recreation Ground in the 1930s. Only one stand has been built, and the surrounding area is not as heavily built up as at present.

highly creditable seventh position out of 18, 13 points behind the champions, Kettering Town, having won 17, drawn five and lost 12 of their 34 games. Undoubtedly the 'find' of the season was Albert Walters who only signed for the side in December, but then proceeded to score 36 goals in the remaining 23 league games, and 63 goals in all games. Sadly, he was to sign for Luton Town at the end of the season.

The following four seasons saw steady if slightly uneven progress, with the highlight undoubtedly being the winning of the Southern League (Eastern Section) Championship in 1930. In those days of teams needing to be elected to the Football League, Aldershot failed by just one vote behind Thames, who ironically were to lose their place in the League to Aldershot just two years later. Strangely, Aldershot's last season in the Southern League was by far their worst, as they finished bottom but one. However, they and Newport County, returning to the League after a one-year gap, were able to capitalise on the demise of Thames in the Third Division (South) and of Wigan Borough's resignation from the Third Division (North) and gain election to the Football League. Once again, the club found themselves having to prepare for a new challenge.

Five years to the day after Aldershot's first game against Grays Thurrock, the club were due to open their campaign in the Football League once more at home to opposition from Essex, this time in the form of Southend United. There the similarities ended for, within three minutes of the kick-off, Aldershot were a goal down and, although they were again level after half an hour, Southend were the eventual winners by two goals to one. Their first season in new company was something of a mixture; in the League they finished 17th out of 22, only seven points better off than Swindon in last place, and a massive 26 points behind champions Brentford. On the other hand, new heights were scaled in the F.A. Cup, where Clapton Orient, Accrington Stanley and Bristol Rovers were all overcome in turn, before Aldershot were drawn away to First Division Derby County, who were eventually to finish seventh in that league. For over an hour, the Aldershot defence held firm, before they conceded two late goals, and tumbled out of the competition. In their first season of league football, Aldershot had reached the last 16 of the F.A. Cup; sadly, it was to be another 46 years before the achievement would be repeated.

The seasons remaining before the Second World War brought a temporary halt to organised football were not marked by any great success; in 1937 Aldershot reached their nadir when they finished nine points adrift at the foot of the League. Beset by financial problems, they were nevertheless re-elected 10 votes ahead of hopeful Ipswich Town. How times change! Two years later, in the last full season before the war, Aldershot attained their highest league finish to date—a creditable 10th, a position not equalled until they finished in the same position in the Fourth Division in 1961. During the same period, the furthest progress made in the F.A. Cup was the third round on three occasions.

While the efforts of the Football Club undoubtedly succeeded in putting the town firmly in the national consciousness, the Aldershot Military Tattoos held throughout the 1920s and 1930s became an established part of the 'Season', in time attracting huge attendances. Although the Tattoos attained their peak in the years between the two world wars, their origins can be traced back to 1894. In May of that year Queen Victoria attended a review of 12,000 troops on Laffans Plain followed by a Torchlight Tattoo in the grounds of the Royal Pavilion, the idea originating with the Duke of Connaught. He had passed the practical arrangements to a Major Mainwaring of the Royal Welsh Fusiliers, who was sufficiently successful in his efforts to leave the Queen 'pleased' with the spectacle (although presumably not amused!).

In Edwardian times the Tattoo bore closer resemblance to a fête than to anything else for, although marching displays and military band music were included, refreshment tents were also provided, as was a fair, complete with a steam-powered roundabout with galloping horses. The last Tattoo before the outbreak of the First World War was held over a period of four days in June 1914 and, apart from the usual military bands and marching displays, also included gymnastic attractions and a demonstration of Highland dancing. By now the event was called 'The Grand Military Searchlight Tattoo' and was attracting ever increasing attendances. After the First World War, the event was revived under the name of 'The Grand Searchlight Tattoo', and was held at Rushmoor Arena for the first time in 1923, having previously been held on Cove Common, Farnborough. An innovation in the Tattoo's new surroundings was the enactment of battle scenes, which in this year was divided into two parts. The first was set roughly fifty years earlier and consisted of a convoy of horse-drawn Army wagons under attack from a force of Zulus, who were eventually beaten off by the defending troops, albeit with heavy losses. The same scene was then repeated, but this time employing modern weapons, with the Zulus this time being comprehensively routed. Encouraged by the success of this enactment, a more ambitious tableau was mounted the following year, and in 1925 the Battle of Waterloo was re-enacted, the first of a series of historical engagements to be portrayed in future years. These included the storming of Badajoz (1928), Waterloo again (1929), Dettingen (1930) and Inkerman (1931). Community

98-101 Scenes from the
Aldershot Military Tattoo in
the years 1929 (*left*), 1930
(*above*), 1931 (*right*) and 1933
(*below*) respectively.

102 Aldershot and District Traction Company laid on fleets of buses each year to ferry passengers from Aldershot Railway Station to the Aldershot Tattoo in Rushmoor Arena. This particular photograph dates from 1930, but the Tattoo would never have been the success it was without the massive behind the scenes organisation of which the transport arrangements were a part.

singing was introduced in 1927 and continued to be a feature in subsequent Tattoos until the Second World War put an end to such events.

During the 20 years from 1919 to 1939 the Tattoo had grown from fairly modest beginnings to an event of truly national significance requiring an immense effort of organisation and planning. That first post-First World War Tattoo attracted the not inconsiderable total of 25,000 spectators; by 1938 the figure had grown to an astonishing 531,850. In order to accommodate these numbers of people, 200 special trains were laid on from places such as Wolverhampton (costing 7s. 3d.), Blackpool (13s.), Manchester (11s.) and Liverpool (11s. 6d.), amongst a host of smaller towns and cities, the trains being met at the

railway station by a fleet of buses to take the visitors to Rushmoor Arena. The 1939 Tattoo lasted from 7 June to 17 June and, in addition to those attending by train, parking had to be found for 71,000 motor vehicles, and this at a time when not many people could afford the luxury of private transport. Inside the Arena, 33 searchlight projectors threw out 3,000 million candle power, and in all there was some 75 miles of electric wiring involved. Five thousand troops were directly involved in the production, and to back them up there were 3,644 administrative staff working in a variety of capacities behind the scenes. A total of 4,032 costumes were used, which, when broken down into individual items of clothing, numbered 55,244!

Vast as the organisational requirements were for the Tattoo, the event would only have attracted a fraction of the spectators had the means to transport them to Rushmoor Arena, situated nearly three miles from the railway station, not been to hand. The Aldershot and District Traction Company would provide hundreds of bus and charabanc journeys between the Arena and nearby towns and railway stations. With the great numbers of spectators attending the event, especially during the 1930s, the few days each year when the Tattoo was being held would have been the busiest time of the year for the company. At the outbreak of hostilities in 1914, the company had just begun to expand, but during the war itself, many of the vehicles were requisitioned for military purposes, and many of the men volunteered or were called to the colours. When peace was restored, the company again began its course of expansion and by 1922 Petersfield, Chichester and Winchester had been added to the list of towns served by company. The 1920s were a period of fierce competition between the larger companies such as the 'Traco' on the one hand, and a host of smaller concerns on the other. It was by no means unknown for the less scrupulous operators to 'steal' passengers by running a service immediately in front and behind a rival bus, so that they could leapfrog their competitor and squeeze him out of his passengers. This situation had virtually ceased by 1930, however, owing largely to the tighter regulations laid down in the Road Traffic Act of that year, and a period of consolidation ensued until the Second World War arrived to disrupt the nation's life in much the same way as had the First World War. Yet within five years of the end of the war, the company was carrying a record number of passengers—52 million—on 372 vehicles.

Undoubtedly, the busiest short term operating periods in the history of the Aldershot and District Traction Company involved the transportation of visitors to the Aldershot Military Tattoo. Less than eleven weeks after the last spectators left Rushmoor Arena following the last Aldershot Military Tattoo, Nazi troops marched into Poland, and the country, with Aldershot well to the fore, once more found itself at war with Germany.

103   The Silver Jubilee Review of the Army by King George V at Rushmoor Arena on 13 July 1935. The East Yorkshire Regiment are passing the saluting base.

104   The waiting room at Aldershot Bus Station pictured in about 1938. Beyond are houses in The Grove. The bus station has now been resited next to the railway station and a residential development has been built on the site.

105   The members of Aldershot Liberal Club pictured in the 1920s before setting off on an outing. Note the barrel of beer and the gentlemen holding beer bottles. In the background is the tower of the brewery.

106 East End School boys' football team pictured in about 1930. Local resident Eric Clifford's father Samuel Clifford is on the back row, extreme left.

107 A view of Manor Park in the 1930s. This scene has changed very little today, and High Street is just visible through a gap in the trees on the left.

108 High Street in the 1920s, looking towards what is now the NAAFI roundabout.

109 High Street looking west towards the Wellington Street junction in the 1920s. The two-storeyed buildings on the left were built in 1857 and are a good example of those built to service the new Camp.

Chapter Six

The Second World War

Twenty-five years earlier, in 1914, Lord Grey of Falloden had uttered his famous phrase about the 'lamps going out all over Europe', and now it seemed that history was repeating itself, except this time more literally, as the demands of the blackout were more stringently enforced. Unlike the period immediately before the First World War, this time it had seemed for some months that a conflict would be inevitable, and to this end preparations were undertaken in Aldershot to meet the coming threat.

Since the Munich Crisis of 1938 the Government had endeavoured to boost the strength of the Armed Forces by introducing a form of conscription for the Militia; this in turn led to the need for additional buildings in which to accommodate the extra men. Although the scale of the construction process was much smaller than had occurred 80 years earlier when the Army first arrived in Aldershot, there were nevertheless comparisons with that earlier time. Workmen poured into the town from the surrounding areas to help build

110 A view across the rooftops taken from the junction of Wellington Street and Union Street. Many of the buildings in the foreground were demolished to make way for Phase II of the Wellington Centre.

the new barracks, and special trains were even laid on from London in order to transport the workmen into the town. By July 1939 the facilities were sufficiently under way, and the first Militia men duly arrived in Aldershot on the 15th of that month; in only seven short weeks Aldershot and the rest of the country would again find itself at war with Germany.

When war was finally declared on 3 September, Aldershot, in common with many other towns across the country, busied itself with taking air-raid precautions. Aldershot was

probably better organised in this area than most places—the A.R.P. wardens had paraded on the Recreation Ground on the same day the first Militia men had arrived—but the declaration of war added a sense of urgency to their activities. In the Camp itself, trenches and shelters which had been dug at the time of the Munich Crisis were enlarged and improved, and plans were made to deal with the threat of attack by gas. In localities around the Camp, gas-proof rooms were constructed, and cleansing stations built; at this early stage of the

war, it was envisaged that Aldershot would be a prime venue for enemy attention. In these first days of hostilities, many of the troops stationed in the town were among those mobilised to join the British Expeditionary Force for service in France.

Perhaps the greatest inpact in Aldershot during the war years would be made by the Canadian troops. One week after Great Britain herself declared war, Canada followed suit, with the first troops arriving in December. It was decided in that month that their headquarters would be in Aldershot, but during the first few months of 1940, they were moved around the country as the perceived needs of the war dictated. First, they were despatched to Scotland in readiness for a planned (but never executed) assault on Norway after the Germans had attacked that country; then they were sent to Dover with the intention of bolstering the troops already in France. That they were destined not to cross the English Channel, in 1940 at any rate, was due to the rapidly worsening situation on the Continent and it was finally

111 The Second World War saw thousands of men pass through Aldershot en route to the various theatres of war around the world. The men pictured left were in the Royal Army Service Corps and are pictured at Clayton Barracks in February 1940.

decided that they could serve no useful purpose there. The evacuation of 338,000 troops from Dunkirk in late May and early June 1940 caused huge problems of accommodation. Many of these men arrived in Aldershot by train, and were housed in barracks, or simply under canvas, again providing an echo of the early tented encampment of 80 years before. This time, the camp was to be of a much more temporary nature, for although some days were to pass before the men could be properly organised and housed, in a relatively short space of time accommodation had been found for them all.

Following the Battle of France, the new Prime Minister, Winston Churchill, warned the country that the Battle of Britain was about to begin, and so it seemed when early air raids, as expected, were carried out on the south coast ports of Southampton and Portsmouth. Aldershot, too, was thought to be a prime target, and on 6 July the first bombs duly fell on the town, and a total of seven people were killed and many more injured as a Heinkel He 111 dropped bombs on Guillemont Barracks, Wellington Avenue, Knollys Road, and Salamanca Barracks. The expected onslaught did not materialise, however, at least as far as Aldershot was concerned. The next attack did not occur for more than three months, when on 11 October a single bomb was dropped at the junction of Cranmore Lane with Farnborough Road, causing two fatalities. Quite why Aldershot never became at this stage a primary target for the Luftwaffe is not clear; perhaps they considered the town to be too

112 A detachment of infantry march along High Street as part of Salute the Soldier Week on 22 July 1944. Civic and military dignitaries are lined up by the flagstaff at the bottom right of the picture.

well prepared to make it worth their while, or perhaps they were simply sticking to their policy of attacking industrial or communications targets; or, as in the case of the Blitz against places such as London or Coventry, perhaps they simply wished to attack larger concentrations of civilians. Another theory is that the German High Command had an eye on the future, and were sizing up Aldershot as the headquarters for the Wehrmacht once the invasion of Great Britain had been successfully accomplished. In any event, Aldershot was left largely alone in this stage of the war and only 28 bombs fell on civilian Aldershot in the entire conflict, injuring 77 civilians and killing just four. Any attack was merely the result of small-scale activity away from the main bombing campaigns.

The year 1940 also saw the formation of the Local Defence Volunteers, who would in due course be known as the Home Guard. Within a month of Anthony Eden making the appeal for volunteers, the Aldershot Platoon was several hundred strong and being trained and drilled by ex-soldiers of the First World War. This enthusiasm was mirrored across the country and by October 1940, only five months after Eden's appeal, the Home Guard numbered a million and a half men. In Aldershot in early September, when the threat of invasion was felt to be at its height, the 600 men of the Aldershot Home Guard were despatched to stand guard over key positions in the town, such as the Gas Works, while another platoon was based on Cargate Avenue, and two more at Eelmoor and Claycart Bridges. With the call to arms of so many new recruits, it was inevitable that Aldershot would become a centre for their training. It should also be remembered that not only were British troops under training at this time, but so were the men from other nations. In addition to the large numbers of Canadians, troops from New Zealand, South Africa and Australia all arrived in Aldershot for their training. French and Polish troops were stationed in the town as well, and although

there were no American troops actually in the Camp itself, there were large numbers of these men in the vicinity and they could often be seen in the town of Aldershot.

One important aspect of life in wartime Britain was the vital role played by the Fire Brigades. In 1939 Aldershot became the District Headquarters for the area covering the towns of Basingstoke, Camberley, Alton, Farnham and Farnborough, the idea being that mutual assistance would be much more readily—and rapidly—available between these places, and others further afield, as the need arose. The benefits of such planning became apparent as early as September 1940 when the District sent nine crews and engines to London, two of them from Aldershot itself. Not all of the places the crews were sent to were particularly local, either, with Plymouth and Manchester both receiving assistance at different times. A system also operated where the crews would be sent on stand-by to the towns likely to need their help and for several weeks the crews were on continual stand-by outside Portsmouth and Southampton.

In August 1942 occurred the famous Dieppe Raid, carried out by just over 6,000 troops of which nearly 5,000 were Canadian, many of whom had been stationed in Aldershot. The value of the raid has long been debated, but in terms of human life the cost was immense; 3,000 men failed to return, either killed or taken prisoner, and many of those who did return were badly injured. Such losses were bound to be keenly felt in a town the size of Aldershot, and whereas before the raid thousands of Canadian troops were to be seen in the town, afterwards the numbers seemed more like hundreds, and many people were never to see some of their Canadian friends again. Even more noticeable were the long lines of ambulances making their way towards the Cambridge Military Hospital where the several hundred wounded were to be treated. For some the agony of not knowing what had happened to husbands or boyfriends would last

113 The Oaks School in Eggars Hill was one of several private schools in Aldershot between the wars. This picture of a group of pupils was taken in about 1930, and the school suffered damage from the doodlebug or V-1 which fell in the area.

until the end of the war. Sadly, many could only properly begin their grieving when the war ended nearly three years later.

In common with other towns across the United Kingdom, Aldershot played its part in raising funds and equipment for the war effort. Warship Week, in February 1942, was marked by a procession through the town involving a detachment from HMS *Collingwood* and a concert held in the Garrison Theatre by the

concert party from HMS *Kestrel*. It also brought Admiral Sir William James to Aldershot to take the salute from the procession. (Sir William was known in naval circles as 'Bubbles' James, because as a five-year old in 1886 he had been the model for Sir John Millais in the famous Pears Soap advert of the curly-headed boy blowing bubbles through a toy pipe; the nickname stuck with him for the rest of his life!) Warship Week was followed by Wings for Victory Week in 1943, the intention being to raise £200,000 for the provision of four Lancaster bombers and 16 troop-carrying gliders. In the event, this figure was surpassed by more than £44,000, which very nearly paid for a fifth Lancaster! This was in addition to a Spitfire, which had already been provided by the town. The following year saw Salute the Soldier Week, which ran from 15 July with the intention of raising £200,000, a figure which many feared would be too high for a town of Aldershot's size, despite the amount raised the previous year. In the event, this amount was comfortably surpassed and a total of £262,684 was collected, more than sufficient to equip a second Paratroop battalion, as well as provide two additional field medical units.

As the tide of war slowly changed in favour of the Allies, so the anticipation grew of opening the 'Second Front', of undertaking the invasion of Western Europe. For towns and villages throughout the South of England, this meant a huge increase in military activity as preparations were put in hand during the early part of 1944; for a town such as Aldershot, although situated at some distance from the Channel ports, this activity was even more marked. In the Camp, barracks were vacated in order to allow in fresh troops who would be sent to France; convoys of military transport and armour passed through the town to marshalling areas in readiness for dispatch to the Continent, and all through the town, rumour and gossip were rife in trying to guess the date and location of the coming invasion. The main roads south of Aldershot in effect became large car parks—or more accurately, tank parks—as these and other vehicles awaited their call to join the invasion force. In Aldershot itself, Grosvenor Road was closed for one 12-hour period in order to allow the 11th Armoured Division to pass along its route.

After D-Day, on 6 June, things became almost unnaturally quiet and empty, at least for

a while. Yet all this was about to change, in a quite alarming way. One week after the invasion of Normandy, the first V-1s, also known as doodlebugs, buzz bombs or flying bombs, were launched at Great Britain, and although the primary target for these pilotless aircraft was London, other locations received their share of attention, too. The figures show that the capital received 2,304 V-1s and counties more directly in the firing line were also heavily

114 Biles baker's shop pictured in about 1946. Standing outside the shop are on the left the manageress Miss Freestone, and on the right Miss Dorothy Tanner. The shop was one of many which had their windows broken by rioting Canadian troops in 1945, and staff were seen handing out bread to customers through their shattered windows.

115 Like other towns, Aldershot was expected to provide its own Civil Defence. The Mayor of Aldershot, Councillor A.H.J. Stroud, is pictured here in 1944 with the Borough Civil Defence staff.

bombarded, with Kent receiving 1,444, and neighbouring Surrey 295. Hampshire received a more modest 80, at least two of which fell on civilian Aldershot, and more on the Camp itself. Nearly 6,000 civilians were killed nationally by these weapons, but Aldershot was lucky insofar as no human life was lost. The first of these bombs fell in June on gardens at Hillside Road, although such details were not made public in order to deny to the Germans information which might have enabled them to improve their accuracy. *The Aldershot News* of 7 July reported that a flying bomb had fallen 'on a garden in the south of England recently', and 'a good deal of damage was done to windows in shops, dwelling houses and a school.' The school mentioned in the report was actually the Girls' County High School in Highfield Avenue, and the girls inside were showered with glass from the destroyed windows. The Oaks private school in Eggars Hill also suffered considerable damage. In all, three people were detained in hospital for 48 hours and a fourth, a young boy, was sent to a specialist hospital for treatment to a wounded eye. Four houses were rendered uninhabitable by the attack and many more suffered varying degrees of less serious destruction. The second flying bomb came down near Cranmore Lane two months later and again caused much damage to property. In all, over 2,000 buildings were damaged in varying degrees of seriousness. Hitler's other 'V' weapon, the V-2, or supersonic rocket, was altogether a much more serious proposition. Travelling faster than the speed of sound, there was no effective defence against this weapon, and although none fell on Aldershot, the original intention of the Nazis had been to target not only London but also Bristol, Southampton, Portsmouth, Winchester and Aldershot. Fortunately, their plans were largely overtaken by events, and although London was repeatedly hit by V-2s, with one incident alone in New Cross claiming 160 lives, none fell on Hampshire at all, and only eight in neighbouring Surrey.

With the invasion of Normandy successfully completed, and in spite of the onslaught from Hitler's 'V' weapons, it was obvious that the war would soon be over, and when the war in Europe finally came to an end in May 1945, there were scenes of rejoicing in the streets similar to those that had taken place 27 years earlier. The spontaneous outpouring of joy and relief was followed by more sedate yet no less heartfelt celebrations which included Victory Parades, street parties, and 'welcome home' parties for returning servicemen and for men who had spent varying lengths of time as prisoners-of-war. Similar scenes were enacted three months later when the war as a whole came to an end after the unconditional surrender of the Japanese. Officially, there were two days of celebrations, Wednesday and Thursday 15 and 16 August, and when the news of Japan's capitulation was made at midnight on Tuesday 14 August by the new Prime Minister, Clement Attlee, a Victory 'V' in fairy lights was quickly set up in St Michael's Road, followed by spontaneous letting off of fireworks and the lighting of bonfires. The following day saw flags and bunting in the streets, but not on the same scale as for VE Day; for one thing the weather was less kind, and for another, there was less time to prepare the celebrations. A baseball match held on the Recreation Ground did attract a large crowd, however, followed by dancing on the Wednesday evening to music provided by two military bands. For those troops being demobbed, dispersal centres had been set up in Waterloo and Talavera Barracks, and many hundreds of thousands of men would spend their last night as British soldiers here in the spring and summer of 1945 before returning to 'civvy street'.

Some troops, however, couldn't get back to civilian life, or at least back home, quickly enough. This was one of the reasons put forward to explain the events of early July, when large numbers of Canadian troops ran riot in the centre of Aldershot, smashing shop windows and generally causing a large amount of damage. The trouble began on the evening of Wednesday 4 July, when a crowd of dissatisfied Canadian soldiers gathered at the foot of Hospital Hill and marched on the Police Station (then in High Street) to try to obtain the release of Canadians thought to be held there. On finding this not to be the case, they moved along Wellington Street, Union Street, High Street and Victoria Road, smashing shop windows as they went. Shortly before midnight they were herded back to barracks, but not before a huge amount of damage had been caused to shop windows and stock inside the shops. The following day saw meetings and appeals to common sense, which, it was hoped, would succeed in defusing the situation. These hopes were to be disappointed, for what happened on the Thursday evening was far worse than anything that occurred on the Wednesday. On this second night, there appeared to be a greater element of organisation involved than previously—the men gathered at the same spot, the foot of Hospital Hill, at the same time as 24 hours earlier, and from there attacked an amusement arcade on the corner of Short Street and High Street, completing the destruction which had been visited upon it on the Wednesday evening, before turning into Union Street, again smashing any windows left unbroken as they went. Goods were thrown into the road and, if they were of suitable size and weight, were used as missiles to break yet more windows. From Union Street they surged onto High Street where officers made vain attempts to persuade the men to return to barracks. Wellington Street, Victoria Road and Station Road were the next to suffer. The stretch of shops on Grosvenor Road from Victoria Road to High Street did not escape the mob's attention either, and nearly two hours had passed before the riot died down. The men did not attack civilians, but any shopkeeper who attempted to defend his property was threatened with violence, and in one case, it

was stated, by a revolver. One reliable eyewitness thought 500 men were involved, and the damage on the Thursday night was estimated to be six times more extensive than that of the previous night. The total cost of the destruction was an estimated £15,000 and 22,000 square feet of glass had been reduced to mere fragments. *The Aldershot News* described the scene on the Friday morning: 'the streets were heaped with glass trampled into thousands of pieces, and damaged clothing, food and other articles from the wrecked windows. The town looked as if there had been a bad air raid.'

It was clear the Canadian authorities had to act quickly and over 100 men were arrested, some to face a court-martial the following month. The ringleaders received custodial sentences ranging from 16 months to four years in length, but genuine attempts were made to address the real grievances of the rioters. The bill for the damage was settled by the Canadian Government and although the riots would not be forgotten, the vast fund of goodwill built up by the Canadians in the previous six years still counted for a great deal. Despite the damage caused to property and to international relations, it was recognised that it was only a small minority who had been behind the mayhem, and at the end of September 1945 the Freedom of the Borough of Aldershot was presented to the Canadian Army Overseas on the Recreation Ground, mirroring a ceremony that had taken place earlier in the month when the Freedom of the Borough was presented to the Hampshire Regiment. Four hundred representatives of the County Regiment paraded through the town and were presented by the Mayor, Alderman White, with a silver casket containing the parchment scroll of the Freedom document. The Canadian presentation followed much the same format, with the important difference that here a whole army was being honoured, the first time a whole army had received the freedom of a borough anywhere in the country. Accordingly, the scale of the

116 Sir Winston Churchill receiving the Freedom Scroll of the Borough of Aldershot in a ceremony held at the *Dorchester Hotel*, London on 6 July 1948.

ceremony was larger; nearly 10,000 Canadian troops attended the presentation, again held on the Recreation Ground.

The Freedom of the Borough was still to be conferred in one more ceremony, although the formal presentation would not take place for nearly three years. The decision had been taken in November 1944 to bestow this honour on Winston Churchill 'in appreciation of the unique and most distinguished service rendered by him on behalf of the nation in the prosecution of the War.' It had not been possible to make the presentation in 1944 or 1945, but the ceremony was eventually held at the

Dorchester Hotel in London on 6 July 1948, at a lunch attended by 400 Aldershot citizens, representing the military and civilian life of the Borough. In his speech of acceptance, Churchill recalled with pleasure the time he had spent as a subaltern in Aldershot in 1894 and 1895. To much amusement he recounted how he had undertaken his first steeplechase on Tweseldown and had finished third in the race—in a field of four. Thus, nearly three years after the end of the Second World War, and with a sense of celebration and enjoyment uppermost, it could be said that a line had finally been drawn under the events of 1939 to 1945.

Chapter Seven

The Post-War Years

The war was now over, and Aldershot, in common with the rest of the nation, was anxious to put the rigours of the war years behind itself, whilst still wishing to remember and honour those that had died in the conflict. Accordingly, a suggestion was put forward to the effect that Aldershot should honour the memory of those who had died in the darkest hours of the war, namely during the great bombing raids on the towns and cities of the nation. As the plans for the memorial took shape, it was decided that stones and masonry from famous buildings destroyed by the Luftwaffe should be incorporated into a Memorial Shrine, and that this should therefore be designated a National Memorial. Invitations were despatched to mayors and lord mayors the length and breadth of the country and 54 responded with the donation of a stone—or stones—from buildings in their borough, which had been destroyed by air attack. Most notably, stones were sent from the old Coventry Cathedral and from the Tower of London, which had suffered the dropping of two bombs which fell near the White Tower, resulting in the deaths of five people. The Memorial itself takes the form of an eight-feet tall figure in Portland stone of Christ under a small dome; the block of stone had been rejected by Sir Christopher Wren when rebuilding St Paul's Cathedral because of an imperfection contained within it, which it was possible to eliminate when sculpting the new figure. The statue was carved by Josephina de Vasconcellos, who both before and after undertaking the Aldershot Memorial had carried out numerous sculptures, many of which are to be found in the country's cathedrals. Two rockeries flank the Memorial, the stones of which are those sent from the bomb-damaged towns and cities of Great Britain. The larger stones are inscribed with the names of the places from which they originate; the Memorial was officially unveiled by the Duchess of Gloucester on 5 May 1950.

If the general public needed an event to take their minds way from the shortages and rationing they still had to face on a daily basis, the wedding of Princess Elizabeth to Prince Philip of Battenberg in 1947 certainly did so most effectively, and the following year the Olympic Games achieved much the same result. In June 1939 the International Olympic Committee had somewhat optimistically awarded the 1944 games to London—even more optimistically the 1940 Olympics were due to have been held in Tokyo. Given that the war had finished less than three years previously, the venues and facilities available were anything but new, and many of the events were held at some distance from the capital. Aldershot was chosen as the venue for the Equestrian events and for the Modern Pentathlon, using local facilities to host the individual elements of these competitions. The Equestrian events were held at the Aldershot Military Stadium, while the Riding, Fencing and Swimming elements of the Pentathlon were

117-119 The shrine was built in Manor Park. The Borough Engineer, Mr. F.W. Taylor, designed this proposed memorial shrine for the Borough after the Second World War, and it consists of a rock garden comprising pieces of bombed buildings donated from 53 cities.

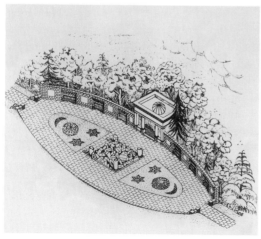

held at Tweseldown, the Gymnasium on Queen's Avenue and in the Municipal Bathing Pool respectively.

A total of nine nations competed in the Equestrian events, although the United Kingdom was not one of them, and the medals were fairly evenly divided amongst them. The individual Grand Prix Jumping event was won by the Mexican Humberto Mariles Cortes on Arete with his compatriot Ruben Uriza on Harvey taking the silver medal. Not surprisingly, Mexico also won the Grand Prix Jumping team event. The individual Three-Day Event gold medal was won by the appropriately named Frenchman Bernard Chevallier on Aiglonne, while the United States won the gold medal in the team event. Controversy overtook the Dressage event, however. The individual gold medal was won by the Swiss Hans Moser on Hummer, but in the team event problems occurred. The Swedes were declared the winners, well ahead of the French, and so the result stood until the following year, when they were disqualified after it was discovered that one of the team members, Gehnall Persson, was not a commissioned army officer as the rules then demanded.

Seventeen nations competed in the Modern Pentathlon, and a special Mayoral Lunch was held at the end of July in the Aldershot and District Traction Company Hall to welcome the competitors. The lunch was attended by representatives from each of the 17 competing countries, as well as by prominent local residents and officials of the Olympic movement. The first element of the Pentathlon was the Riding event, held at Tweseldown racecourse, comprising a 5,000-metre course containing 22 jumps. The riders set off at five-minute intervals and nine of the 45 competitors scored maximum points. The next day saw the Fencing events in the Army School of Physical Training at Fox Gymnasium, and again there was a tie for first place, this time between Captain Willie Grut of Sweden and Lieutenant Morrot Coelho of Brazil. The Shooting events

120   The centrepiece of the shrine in Manor Park is a statue depicting Christ stilling the storm.

were held the next day at Bisley, followed by the Swimming event in the Municipal Bathing Pool in Aldershot Park, where Willie Grut was again successful. The final event of the Pentathlon was the cross-country run of 4,000 metres, the winner being Lieutenant K. Wehlin of Sweden. The winner of the gold medal overall by a huge margin was Wille Grut, who, having won three of the five events, is still widely considered to be the greatest pentathlete of all time.

Six years later, in 1954, saw the beginning of a year of events designed to celebrate the centenary of the arrival of the Army. As no exact date could be established marking the

121 The Town Hall on Grosvenor Road has borne witness to many official ceremonies, and here the Proclamation of the Accession of Queen Elizabeth II is being read on 8 February 1952. The Guard of Honour is provided by the 4th Training Regiment, the Royal Engineers.

122 The Military Centenary of Aldershot was celebrated in 1954. Here is a section of the 3,000 troops marching past the saluting base adjacent to the Town Hall, Grosvenor Road, led by the Royal Artillery Band.

arrival of the Army, it was decided to hold a series of events, spread over the period from April 1954 to April 1955 which in their different ways would mark the anniversary. The programme began with the Mayoral Ball, held at the Officers' Club on Tuesday 20 April. This was in itself a departure from the norm insofar as this was the first occasion the Ball had not been held in civilian Aldershot, and it was followed the next day by arguably the most impressive event in the year's activities. A Ceremonial March, starting from Corunna Barracks Square, followed a route of more than four miles along Hospital Hill, Barrack Road, High Street and Victoria Road before culminating at the viewing platform in Grosvenor Road outside the entrance to the Municipal

Gardens. A total of 3,500 troops, in four contingents six abreast, accompanied by no less than eight military bands were enthusiastically greeted by large crowds along the length of the route. The marching men were made up of young National Servicemen and *The Aldershot News* stated that 'they marched with the precision of seasoned troops' in a 'picture of perfection'. In the evening, a floodlit football match was held at the Recreation Ground between The Army and Aldershot Football Club, with the Army team, which was made up of a team of 'well-known professionals' doing their National Service, running out the winners by two goals to nil. The match was televised by the BBC, which in itself was something of an event, whilst the fact that the

123 The ceremony of beating the bounds at Weybourne Road on 26 June 1954. The actual boundaries of Aldershot had changed very little since the arrival of the Army a century earlier.

game was played under floodlights was also something of a novelty at that time.

Other events in the year included the centenary carnival procession on 26 June, which was followed by a Charity Gala held at the Municipal Bathing Pool. On the same day the ceremony of 'Beating the Bounds' was held, the origins of which are lost in the mists of time. Suffice it to say that a procession of local clergy and other lay officials would mark the boundaries of the parish by beating the boundary stones with sticks of willow in days when maps were either non-existent or too unreliable to be of much use in such matters. The boundaries of Aldershot in 1954 were actually very little different from the boundaries of the area known as 'Aldershott' 100 years previously. Other attractions during the year were the Aldershot Show in Rushmoor Arena in August, a parade of the Old Contemptibles in the same month, and the Trade and Industries Fair, organised by the Chamber of Commerce in Manor Park in September, and attended by 29 local companies. The final event of the year was the unveiling of a Commemorative Fountain in the Prince's Gardens on 5 June 1955, a ceremony which would have been carried out by Her Majesty The Queen ten

days earlier but for the Government who had been inconsiderate enough to call a General Election to take place on that day, which necessitated her presence in London.

One event which occurred during this year of celebration had its origins over thirty years previously when suggestions were first put forward for the establishment of a Public Library in the town. Finally, in April 1953, the Council agreed to the proposals being put forward at that time, and they were put into practice with such effect that the opening ceremony for the new building was able to be held on 23 June 1954. Under the guidance of the first—and only—Borough Librarian, Mr. W.E. French, the service quickly outgrew its premises and in 1961 plans were put into action to add a second storey to the building. This necessitated a complete removal from the building for a period of two years, during which time the service was provided from the former Sergeant's Mess of Warburg Barracks. These premises were far from ideal and far from warm, and during the extremely cold winter of 1962-3 members of staff were frequently sent into the derelict wing of the building to rip up a few more floorboards to throw on the fire! Upon returning to the newly extended building, the library was able to provide two meetings rooms and a much larger reference library, which is now occupied by an extensive collection of books relating to the British Army. Eleven years later the responsibility for providing the library service passed to Hampshire County Council.

In 1961 occurred an event, which closely mirrored the occasion which had taken place nearly seventy years earlier when Charlie Chaplin had taken the first steps on his long and illustrious career; in December 1961, a little known pop group from Liverpool were to make their first live performance in the south of England. The Liverpool promoter Sam Leach had come to the conclusion that the Beatles needed to be seen by London agents and record companies if their career was to progress, so on the principle of Mohammed visiting the mountain, the group were booked to appear at the Palais Ballroom, Queen's Road on the evening of Saturday 9 December. Quite why Aldershot, situated nearly forty miles from London, was chosen is not altogether clear,

but the situation grew worse when no advertisement for the event was placed in *The Aldershot News*. After a gruelling nine-hour journey by van from Liverpool, the Beatles were faced with the prospect of playing to an empty hall. The only solution was to tour the coffee bars and pubs of the town to advertise the event 'on the hoof'; this succeeded in producing a grand total of 18 customers, who, despite the sparse attendance were nevertheless valiantly entertained by the group. The event had been advertised as a 'Battle of the Bands' between the Beatles and a long since forgotten group rejoicing in the name of Ivor Jay and the Jay-walkers, and was originally intended to be the first of five such contests. The following week, the battle was between Ivor Jay's band again and another Liverpool outfit called Rory Storm and the Hurricanes, which on this occasion, with the benefit of an advertisement in *The Aldershot News*, attracted over 200 paying customers. By an ironic twist of fate, Rory Storm's drummer, one Ringo Starr, was soon

124 In 1954 the first public library was opened in Aldershot. Built and funded by the Borough Council it was originally a single-storey edifice which soon proved to be too small to serve the Borough's needs and was doubled in size in 1963.

125 The opening ceremony of the Public Library on 23 June 1954. From left to right are: Mrs. A. Colvin, Miss R.A. Benoit (Committee Clerk), Mrs. Crosby (of Crosby Builders), Mr. F.W. Taylor (Borough Surveyor), Alderman W.E. Eddy, Alderman J. Drew, Alderman F. Stay, Mr. H. Sales (Town Clerk), Mr. W.E. French (Borough Librarian) and Rev. T.H. Dart (vicar of Aldershot).

126 Aldershot's one and only Borough Librarian, Mr. W.E. French, pictured in his office in 1965. Mr. French served as Borough Librarian from the Library's opening in 1954 until Hampshire County Council took over the running of the service 20 years later.

to replace the Beatles' then drummer, Pete Best, just in time for the band's first single release.

At about the time of the Beatles' appearance in Aldershot, the military town began to undergo a change almost as drastic as that which had taken place a century earlier. The barracks built between the 1850s and the 1890s had remained largely unaltered through numerous colonial wars, the Boer War and two world wars, but it was now felt that the needs of a modern army could best be met in a manner very different from that of the previous century. One of the major changes envisaged was the separation of living quarters from the working environment of the army; hitherto, barracks had been sited adjacent to parade grounds whereas now they would be located on the edge of the military town, closer to civilian facilities, which, it was hoped, would lead to better integration. In order to achieve such a bold reorganisation, it was recognised that, rather than tackling the matter in a piecemeal manner, the entire locality would need to be considered. In practical terms, this meant that virtually everything would have to be demolished and rebuilt at a cost of an estimated £50 million in a programme expected to last from 10 to 15 years.

Work began in 1959 and the demolition of Warburg Barracks was followed by that of Willems, Badajos, Salamanca, Talavera and Waterloo Barracks, all of which, with the exception of the Warburg site, were to become estates of married quarters. The Warburg site was acquired by the Borough Council, and was in due course to become the location for the Prince's Hall, the Health Centre, Magistrates' Court and Police Station. The first of the new married quarters in Talavera Park was completed in 1964 and comprised a mixture of smaller houses and maisonettes reflecting the need for accommodation that would be cheap and easy to maintain. The housing in Willems Park was of a different design, consisting of a series of maisonettes, many of which were in six- and eight-storey blocks. In addi-

tion to the demolition of many of the old Victorian buildings, the layout of the road system was also destined to undergo a big change. Alison's Road was created and passed under the Farnborough Road; once this was completed, many of the feeder roads onto the Farnborough Road were closed, leaving just three points of access: one at Alison's Road and one each at the junctions with Lynchford Road in North Camp and with a newly constructed Wellington Avenue adjacent to Willems Park. This latter development went hand in hand with the closure in May 1969 of the original course of Wellington Avenue, which had joined the Farnborough Road opposite All Saints' Church. The importance of landscaping was not forgotten in the master plan and over 100,000 trees and shrubs were planted in and around the Military Town.

The rebuilding of the Military Town was undoubtedly necessary from the point of view of providing a viable, efficient working environment for the Army, and it is impossible to live in a museum, but, nevertheless, the feeling still remains that by sweeping away so much of the original Victorian architecture Aldershot suffered a net loss rather than a net gain. Aldershot was in effect a Victorian 'new town', conceived, planned and built in a 40-year period, and many of the old buildings that were swept away could perhaps have been adapted to more modern purposes without the need for total demolition. The Officers' Mess Block, Warburg Barracks are a case in point. Sold by the Army to the Borough Council, could they not have been converted for use as the Magistrates' Court, or perhaps used as Council Offices in which case there might have been no need to build expensive new accommodation for Rushmoor Borough Council in Farnborough a decade or so later? It *is* easy to be wise with the benefit of hindsight, and it should not be forgotten that in the early 1960s Victorian architecture was being torn down the length and breadth of the country, but if the building of Willems Park and Talavera Park

127 The early 1960s saw much demolition and rebuilding of both civilian and military Aldershot. The Hippodrome Theatre was demolished and replaced by an office building with shops beneath in Hippodrome House. In this picture of July 1961 the Gale and Polden building, itself to be demolished in the 1980s, can also be seen.

128 Opposite the library stood the NAAFI Club, pictured here in 1958 while undergoing alterations. The site is now occupied by the fast food restaurant Burger King.

129   A view looking over the bus station towards the railway station in the 1950s. With the exception of the railway station itself, nearly all the buildings in the photograph have since been demolished.

130   On 4 October 1962 Mr. James Ramsden, Parliamentary Under Secretary of State for War, unveiled this commemoration stone to mark the rebuilding of the barracks in Aldershot Military Town. It weighs 70 tons, and is 76 feet 9 inches long, incorporating a quantity of crushed brick and rubble from the old demolished barracks.

131   A view of 1962 showing the extent of the rebuilding operations in the Military Town. The diamond–shaped building on the left became the NAAFI while the empty area behind was to make way for new housing developments.

132   Civilian Aldershot meets Military Aldershot in 1962. Talavera Park is in the course of construction in the foreground, while well-known landmarks in the civilian town include the water tower, top left, and the Grosvenor Road Methodist Church tower a little further to the right.

133   *Top.* A 1966 view showing the new Willems Park under contruction in the midst of what looks like a swathe of destruction. Wellington Avenue still runs arrow-straight towards the Red Church, but its future route can be traced in the diversion it makes to the left across the building site.

134   *Above.* The imposing façade of the Officers' Mess of Willems Barracks photographed in the early 1900s. This and many other similar buildings were swept away in the redevelopment of the 1960s.

135   *Right.* The Officers' Mess at Beaumont Barracks, photographed in 1974, has obviously seen better days, and has since been demolished.

136 A view looking across the Prince's Gardens towards Hospital Hill and Talavera Barracks. The Prince's Gardens were the site of the first Royal Engineers' Camp in 1853 prior to the establishment of the permanent camp.

137 A very different view across the Prince's Gardens. The Prince's Hall is just visible on the left, while the old Talavera Barracks have been replaced by modern maisonettes, which were in turn replaced by new houses in the 1990s.

was the answer in the 1960s, why were they in turn demolished a mere 30 years later?

One of the most tragic occurrences in the history of Aldershot took place on Tuesday, 22 February 1972 when the Official IRA detonated a bomb at the Officers' Mess of the Headquarters of the 16th Parachute Brigade in Pennefathers Road. Seven people, all civilians, were killed and many more injured in the attack which was 'justified' by the IRA as retaliation for the deaths of 13 civilians killed in the 'Bloody Sunday' riots which had occurred just over three weeks earlier. The bomb, which comprised 50 pounds of gelignite left in a Ford Cortina, detonated at twenty minutes to one in the afternoon. In addition to the seven dead, which included five women, a Roman Catholic priest and a 58-year-old gardener, 16 people were treated in the Cambridge Military Hospital, and five of those were still receiving treatment three days later. The IRA's expression of regret that civilians had been killed was less than convincing: 'The target was military and if the British authorities want to use civilians as stool pigeons the responsibility lies with them.' Despite all the evidence to the contrary, the leadership of the IRA was still claiming some days after the explosion that 12 officers had been killed and the amount of explosives used was five times greater than was actually

138 Hospital Hill in 1951 showing Warburg Barracks outside of which is a passing lorry. The building on the right corner of Wellington Avenue was used as the Council's Housing Department at the time the photograph was taken.

139 As part of the Borough's Golden Jubilee celebrations in 1972, the Mayor, Mrs. V. Nevett, is seen presenting the Miss Aldershot prize to Mrs. Annette Hall at Aldershot Manor School on 21 June.

the case. In terms of damage caused to buildings, debris from the Mess and the car used in the attack rained down on buildings as much as 300 yards away and windows of shops in High Street nearly half a mile distant were also shattered by the blast. A plume of grey-brown smoke rose over the scene where the pile of rubble extended up to the level of what had been the ground floor ceiling.

The response of the emergency services was quick and efficient, and within 10 minutes police and troops had cordoned off the Camp.

Ambulances and fire engines also arrived quickly at the scene and began helping those who were digging at the rubble with their bare hands in an attempt to rescue the injured. Grey concrete dust covered everything, and soon settled on the rescue workers with the result that sometimes it was difficult to distinguish between the rescuers and the rescued. By Wednesday, the day after the explosion, more than 150 extra police had been brought into Aldershot and an inquiry squad set up. The number of uniformed policemen in the town was also increased to 200 in number, and in due course three men, Noel Thomas Jenkinson, Michael Francis Duignan and Francis Finbar Kissane, were arrested in London and remanded in custody, charged with causing the explosion. Two months after the blast, the evidence was sent to the Director of Public Prosecutions and in October the trial of the three men began at Winchester Crown Court. On the twentieth day of the trial, 14 November 1972, Jenkinson was sentenced to life imprisonment with a recommendation that he should serve not less than 30 years, while Kissane was acquitted of the murders but sentenced to two years in jail for conspiring with Duignan to pervert the course of justice. Duignan received three years for possessing an unlicensed shotgun and a further six months for conspiring to pervert the course of justice.

Thus ended one of the worst occurrences in the history of Aldershot, although for the families of the bereaved, or for those involved in the explosion, the events of February 1972 would remain with them for the rest of their lives.

Chapter Eight

Aldershot—Past, Present and Future

The first half of the 1970s was a time when local government circles the length and breadth of the country were forced to take an intense interest in the recommendations of the Redcliffe Maud Report. Actually published in the summer of 1969, the implications for Aldershot would be far reaching indeed, forcing the town into a marriage of convenience with its near neighbour Farnborough. The idea of merging the two towns was not a new one, having first been proposed before the Second World War, but now, following the Local Government Act of 1972, the proposals were about to become reality. The name of the new local authority was chosen from more than

300 suggestions made by members of the general public, and the one chosen was 'Rushmoor', selected at least partly to reflect the nearby location of Rushmoor Arena, home of the Aldershot Military Tattoos before the Second World War.

The transition from Aldershot Borough Council to Rushmoor Borough Council was marked on 31 March 1974—the final day before the new authority came into being—by a ceremony held in the Prince's Gardens opposite the Prince's Hall. At five o'clock in the afternoon the Borough's flag was flown from the flagpole in the Gardens, and a military band beat the retreat, before the Mayor spoke

140 The Prince's Hall photographed in about 1974, shortly after it opened. Situated on the site of the Warburg Barracks, the hall has been the venue for many concerts, meetings, exhibitions, pantomimes and civic ceremonies.

119

141 A good example of 1960s architecture. Between the Health Centre on the left, and the Law Courts on the right, can be seen the rectangular shape of Willems Park Army quarters, happily since demolished to make way for Tesco's supermarket.

142 More than one military organisation has been granted the Freedom of the Borough and the Parachute Regiment was honoured in this way in 1963.

143 Aldershot Market pictured in 1965. Situated off Victoria Road, the site is now the home of the Wellington Centre, while the market itself is housed on the ground floor of the multi-storey car park on High Street.

a few words to the crowd, followed by prayers spoken by the Mayor's Chaplain. The flag was then lowered for the last time, and the Honorary Remembrancer of the Borough, Lt.-Col. Howard Cole then spoke a few well-chosen words:

> This evening we have watched an event which is a milestone in our local history. It has taken place on an historic site, for here, where we stand, was erected in the autumn of 1853 the camp for the party of Royal Engineers which came to survey and lay out the military camp which has grown into the military town ... After today the Borough ceases to exist but, proud of its past, and proud of its 120 years close association with the Army—the name of the town will live on!

The folded flag was then presented by the Mayor to Lt.-Col. Cole who bore it across the road to the Prince's Hall, from the steps of which the Mayor took the salute. A reception

attended by past mayors of the borough, the Commander of Aldershot Garrison, Aldershot's M.P., Julian Critchley and representatives from other local organisations was then held in the Prince's Hall, and so the Borough of Aldershot had effectively ceased to exist.

Following the wholesale developments which had taken place in the Military Town a decade or so earlier, it was recognised in the early 1960s that in order to maintain the town's position as an important local shopping centre, a large portion of the central area would need to be substantially redeveloped. This area was bounded by Union Street, Cross Street, Victoria Road and Wellington Street and included many long-established Aldershot enterprises, as well as the site of Aldershot Market. The responsibility for the scheme passed from Aldershot Borough Council to the new Rushmoor Borough Council in April 1974 and in the following June work on the site formally

144 The Victoria Road entrance to the market, in 1974.

145 A bird's-eye view of the town centre in 1975. Work on building the Wellington Centre has yet to start, although the site has been cleared in readiness for its construction.

commenced. The topping out ceremony was performed in July 1977 by the Mayor of Rushmoor, Councillor W.E. Farthing, and on 13 November 1978 the doors of the development, by now known as the Wellington Centre, were opened to the public. The Duke of Wellington himself officiated at the formal opening of the centre which took place on 30 April 1979. In tandem with the new development, Union Street and Wellington Street were both pedestrianised, making those areas of the town centre much more pleasant.

Phase Two of the Wellington Centre moved forward much less smoothly when it was being built between 1988 and 1992. This involved building a huge multi-storey car park on the site of the old police houses on High Street, incorporating in the ground floor of the car park a home for the Market, whose stallholders had been using the site since losing their old home to the original Wellington Centre. The shops in Phase Two extended towards, but not as far as, the buildings on Station Road, with an entrance on High Street opposite the new car park. Much of the area earmarked for development as Phase Two of the Wellington Centre had been used as a car park, which now being unavailable meant that there were considerably fewer car parking spaces available in the town centre. This was bad enough in itself, but when the company financing the development collapsed, work was suspended on the project for more than 12 months. By the time the Centre was finally completed in 1992 many people had lost the habit of using Aldershot as a shopping centre, preferring to visit places such as Guildford or Camberley, who had also been developing their shopping centres, but without the problems experienced in Aldershot. To compound the problem, many of the units in the new part of the Wellington Centre remained unoccupied, contributing to a general feeling of decline. The situation was turned around in October 1999, however, with the redesignation of the newer half of the Wellington Centre as 'The Galleries' where a series of designer goods and clothes shops were opened.

146 The Arcade ran between Wellington Street and Victoria Road. In this picture of its interior taken in 1961 there are the shops of Eaton's stationers, Burnett's shoe repairers, the Southern Bookshop, Simes' leather goods, Hedley Barrett opticians on the left hand side, and on the right are the premises of the Shamrock Linen Warehouse.

147 The Arcade was demolished to be replaced by a pastiche of the Victorian original in which many of the shops remained empty for several years. This is a view of the Victoria Road entrance.

148 The Wellington Centre Phase Two, showing the High Street entrance of the shopping centre leading to the new 'Galleries' development of 1999.

149   The High Street in 2000. The Police Station and houses have been replaced by a multistorey car park where the weekly market is held on the ground floor, thus continuing the long tradition of the market in Aldershot.

150   The Officers' Club has now been redeveloped as *Potter's International Hotel*. The core of the original still exists, surrounded by the new sections of the building.

151 The rear of *Potter's International Hotel* showing its sports hall. The Army Cricket Club field still exists in the foreground and part of the complex is still used as the Officers' Sports Club.

The early 1970s also saw a brief upturn in the fortunes of Aldershot Football Club. At the end of the 1972/3 season they finished in fourth position in the Fourth Division, thus earning their first promotion since obtaining League status 41 years earlier. Their newly won status lasted for just three seasons before they found themselves being relegated back to the Fourth Division, but in 1987 their fortunes again seemed to be on the up when they defeated the once mighty Wolverhampton Wanderers home and away in the end of season play-offs for a place in the Third Division. This time their stay in more exalted company

was to last just two seasons, and the writing was on the wall with regard to their financial situation. In the wake of the Bradford fire and Heysel Stadium disasters, safety work costing £300,000 was carried out at the Recreation Ground, and when one of the contractors was not paid, he filed a petition for a winding-up order. Two months later, in April 1988, the Inland Revenue weighed in with a bill for £70,000 which had to be paid within six days, and it was clear that the situation was becoming increasingly desperate. The end appeared to have been reached on 31 July 1990 when the club was officially wound up in the High Court with over £150,000 owing to the Inland Revenue.

There then followed one of the more bizarre episodes in the history of any football club when they were rescued by a 19-year-old 'entrepreneur' named Spencer Trethewy who pledged £200,000 to save the club. This injection of cash enabled the club to struggle on, but questions were already being asked about Trethewy's *bona fides* when he was suspended from the board following allegations in the national press concerning the origins of his money. It later transpired that his money was borrowed and in 1994 he was convicted on a string of fraud charges in the course of which he had tricked hotels out of several thousand pounds. Nevertheless, whether he had the money or not, Trethewy's intervention did enable the club to survive in the Football League for nearly two more seasons. The end came towards the end of the 1991/2 season in March when £350,000 was needed to rescind a winding-up order lodged seven weeks earlier by the Inland Revenue. The club were expelled from the Football League and locked out of the Recreation Ground by Rushmoor Borough Council in a move designed to protect the Council's own position. The end came as something of a relief to the players who had not been paid for several months; the demise of the club at least meant they could sign on the dole or seek positions with other clubs.

Although Aldershot was dead, it was a case of long live Aldershot Town. A new club was founded in the summer an accepted into the Diadora League Division Three in time for the start of the 1992/3 season. The Recreation Ground was cleared by Rushmoor to be their home and the stated aim was to regain their Football League status in 10 years. This may have seemed something of a tall order as it would entail five promotions, but the first two were achieved in the first two seasons, and spurred on by a level of support which was not far below that of their Football League days, they are still on course to fulfil that aim.

The logo of the new club features a phoenix rising from the ashes, an appropriate emblem in the circumstances, which was designed by the new club's founding president, the comic actor Arthur English who was a life-long supporter of the 'Shots'.

As early as 1960 it was becoming apparent that one of the major problems facing the area was traffic congestion, and that some form of relief measures would be necessary if the town centres of Aldershot and Farnborough and the communities in the Blackwater Valley were not to become gridlocked. It was not until the mid-1980s, however, that the project was seriously considered and the decision was taken to link the M3 at Frimley with the A31 at Runfold, following the course of the River Blackwater for much of its length. The road was to be built in three sections, North, South and Centre, with the two end sections getting underway first in March 1992, and opening two years later; the Southern section also involved constructing a stretch of dual carriageway on the A31, the Hog's Back. The Central section was the final piece in the jigsaw and work commenced on this in June 1994. This section was more difficult to complete than either of the other two, involving the construction of several bridges over the new road, including an aqueduct 134 metres long carrying the Basingstoke Canal over the road. Much of the road lay below the natural water level in the area, which necessitated special regard to drainage matters and the River Blackwater itself was re-routed for several hundred yards. The final section of the road was officially opened on 19 July 1996, the whole eight-mile road having cost £135 million. The benefits to local communities were immediately noticeable, with many areas experiencing a drop of one third in their traffic levels. Another effect of the construction of the road meant that hitherto inaccessible locations now had greater access to the motorway network at Frimley, leading to a welcome boost to the local economies.

As the 20th century gives way to the 21st, the town finds itself at something of a crossroads. To say that Aldershot lost its identity in 1974 when control over its own affairs passed to Rushmoor Borough Council is clearly not true, but certainly the feeling of being in control of its own destiny was greatly reduced. It is, in any case, too simplistic to blame Rushmoor for all Aldershot's ills; Rushmoor performs its duties as efficiently as any district or borough council and, in any case, some of the services provided by the old Aldershot Borough Council—such as the Public Library—passed to Hampshire County Council; but few would argue with the notion that Aldershot has been in a slow but steady decline for the last 30 or 40 years. Whether a small Aldershot Municipal Borough such as existed prior to 1974 would have been able to continue providing its services in the harsher economic climate of the 1970s and 1980s is something we shall never know, but perhaps a greater sense of civic pride and identity might have meant a more sympathetic approach to some of the issues facing the town during the past two and a half decades.

The destruction of many of the old Victorian buildings is something to be regretted, both in the Military Town and in the civilian one. The demolition of the arcade joining Wellington Street to Victoria Road, only to be replaced by a new pseudo-Victorian substitute, is a case in point. Surely, the old arcade could have been refurbished at a fraction of the cost, and Aldershot would still have had a reminder of its Victorian past? In some respects, however, it is pointless to look back on past mistakes or missed opportunities—it is the future which must now concern us. To a degree, Aldershot has to re-invent itself and face up to new challenges posed by developments elsewhere in the region. Other towns perhaps have better facilities to offer the public and periodic reports in the press of the Army leaving Aldershot altogether mean the future sometimes looks more than a little uncertain.

Yet the infrastructure is in place to enable the town to move forward. The Blackwater Valley Relief road means the town now has better communications with the outside world than at any time in its history; a compact and well laid-out shopping centre is in the town's favour, and if the Army were to leave the area, there would at least be no shortage of available land. An article published in *The Sunday Times* in March 2000 reported that the Army were considering leaving the Aldershot area entirely as part of a money-saving exercise; land in Yorkshire and Scotland was considerably cheaper than in the south of England, where it was valued at £1.1 million per acre. The Government had indeed invested wisely in the light of the original purchase price of £12 per acre for Aldershot Heath in 1854!

Aldershot has come a long way in a relatively short space of time. The villagers of 1854—many of whose descendants still live locally—who witnessed the arrival of the first troops were doubtless astonished at the rapid transformation which was visited on their village of 'Aldershott'. The challenge now is to ensure the town of Aldershot continues to thrive in the 21st century and beyond.

Bibliography

The Aldershot News

Association of Football Statisticians, *The Statistics of Aldershot Football Club* (1982)

Baigent, Francis Joseph, *A Collection of records and documents relating to the* Hundred and Manor of Crondall in the County of *Southampton, part 1: Historical and Manorial* (1891)

Bankoff, George, *The Story of Plastic Surgery* (1952)

Censuses—1841, 1851, 1861, 1871, 1881, 1891

Chaplin, Charles, *My Autobiography* (1964)

Childerhouse, Tim, *Book of Aldershot* (1992)

Childerhouse, Tim, *Bygone Aldershot* (1984)

Cole, H., *The Story of Aldershot,* 2nd edn. (1980)

Daniell, Georgina, *Aldershot: a record of Mrs. Daniell's work amongst soldiers and its sequel* (1879)

Dictionary of National Biography

Greenberg, Stan, *The Guinness Olympics Fact Book* (1991)

Holmes, Peter, *Aldershot's Buses* (1992)

Killanin (Lord) and Rodda, John (eds.), *The Olympic Games* (1976)

Lewisohn, Mark, *The Complete Beatles Chronicle* (1992)

Longmate, Norman, *The Doodlebugs* (1981)

Longmate, Norman, *Hitler's Rockets* (1985)

Maclay, Mark, *Aldershot's Canadians in Love and War, 1939-45* (1997)

Phillips, Stephen and Owen, Vivienne, *Images of Aldershot* (1998)

Robinson, John Martin, *The Wyatts: an architectural dynasty* (1979)

Rollin, Jack, *The History of Aldershot Football Club, 1926-1975* (1975)

Sheldrake, W., *A Guide to Aldershot and its Neighbourhood* (1859)

Sheldrake's Aldershot Military Gazette

Townsin, Alan, *The Best of British Buses, No. 4, 75 years of Aldershot and District* (1981)

Vickers, Paul H., *'A Gift so Graciously Bestowed': the History of the Prince Consort's Library* (1993)

Vine, P.A.L., *London's Lost Route to Basingstoke* (1968)

Walters, John, *Aldershot Review* (1970)

Williams, R.A., *The London and South Western Railway, volume 2: Growth and Consolidation* (1973)

Young, Mrs., *Aldershot and all about it* (1857)

Index

Numbers in **bold** refer to the page numbers of illustrations

The centre of 'Aldershott' as shown on a map of 1871. It is only 17 years since the Army first arrived yet already the town has grown considerably. The railway station, bottom right, is isolated in what was open country and a lot of the area to the east of Grosvenor Road, then still known as Bank Street is still to be developed.